Daughters of Dunn House 1953:

Stories of Fisk Early Entrants

Hildred Roach
Donna Penn Towns
Maryann Rebecca Gay Rozzell
Jeanne Joyce Johns Adkins
Barbara Laverne Crockett Dease
Jane Geraldine Fort
Ellena Auxvasse Stone Huckaby

Dorrance Publishing Co
585 Alpha Drive
Suite 103
Pittsburgh, PA 15238
Visit our website at *www.dorrancebookstore.com*

ISBN: 979-8-88683-639-4
eISBN: 979-8-88683-640-0

Acknowledgments

The authors of these narratives extend their most sincere gratitude to the gracious persons who proofread our stories, and who gave us their clever critiques, perceptive edits, advisements and technical assistance. Assistance from Judith Korey, Callye Christopher, David S. Donaldson, Liane Rozzell, Sékou Writes, Tommyzee Tinsley, Patricia Carter, Helen Flagg, Marlene Brooks, Amy Adkins Harris, Mitzi Paige, and Joi Collette Rideout was all on point, practical and professional, and therefore supplied invaluable credence and support to the weight and worth of this project. Special thanks are also extended to Brenda McDonald, Nicole Suprak and Danielle Pendzich, Dorrance Publishing staff.

It goes without saying that the completion of these true stories stands as a tribute to our alma mater Fisk University, the Ford Foundation, mentors from fraternities and sororities, our families and other supporters who cheered us along the way.

In Memoriam of Those Who Began with Us and Left All Too Soon

Marlena Donnette Crippens McMillan
Helen Harris McDuffy
Carol Pindle Smith
Dr. Niara Sudarkasa (né Gloria Marshall)
Jacquelyn Walton Sadler

Contents

Preface

Dunn House afforded a lifetime of memories to the young teenage girls who entered its portals in the fall of 1953. It was to be a first-year home for girls entering the Basic College program at Fisk University in Nashville, Tennessee. The Basic College was a Ford Foundation project based on the premise that the last two years of high school were merely repeated in the first two years of college and that talented students could skip those years and proceed straight from the 10th and 11th grades of high school into college. Twelve Universities across the country participated in the "Early Entrant Program," as it was called. Fisk University and Morehouse College were the only two Historically Black Colleges and Universities (HBCUs) in the program.

Fisk was founded six months after the end of slavery in 1865 by three members of the American Missionary Association: John Ogden, the Reverend Erastus Milo Cravath, and the Reverend Edward P. Smith. It was named in honor of General Clinton B. Fisk of the Tennessee Freedmen's Bureau, who provided the facilities from former army barracks. It was designed to cater to the former slaves who showed ability to function on a more intellectual level than the laborers that Booker T. Washington promoted. It catered more to what W.E.B. DuBois later referred to as "The Talented Tenth." DuBois, in fact, attended Fisk University before moving on to Harvard University.

This is about the Fisk experience and the effect it had on lives beyond the seven whose true narratives are told here, and covers the African-American girls who attended Fisk's Basic College, back in the era now called "The Silent Generation." This was the era before the sit-ins and racial protests led by Martin Luther King Jr.

The girls graduated, attended graduate schools and became administrators and professors of universities, lawyers, anthropologists, physical therapists, editors, psychologists, art curators and the like. They all attribute the successes they have experienced in their lives to the days at Fisk University and particularly to that first year together at Dunn House.

Dunn House was a two-story, eight-bedroom house that sat on 17th Street in the middle of the campus, across from a beautiful magnolia grove and a few yards away from the Basic College boys' dormitory, which housed the males in the Early Entrant Program. Mrs. Holtzclaw, called "Mother Holtz" by the girls, was in charge of the girls and assigned roommates according to her concept of compatibility. Some of the girls later pondered over her choice of pairing: Jane, Jacquie and Marlena (the Nashvilleans); Jeanne and Carol (the Alabamans); Hildred and Barbara (the N. Carolinians); Gloria and Helen (the Floridians); Jackie and Donna (the dentist's and doctor's daughters); Maryann, Ellena and Eva (no one could figure out). While all the girls were compatible, close friendships developed among them with no regard to roommate status and still exist to this day.

In the following pages, seven of the Dunn House Girls, as they came to call themselves after a reunion in 2000, tell their stories. It is a tribute to Fisk University, the Ford Foundation, and to the lasting legacy that was implanted in its students, now octogenarians, who remain "ever on the altar."

Donna Penn Towns, Ph.D., Attorney-at-Law, retired
Silver Spring, MD
September 2021

Donna Penn Towns

I guess you could say that Fisk was in my genes from the start. My father had attended Meharry Medical College, whose campus is adjacent to the Fisk campus, as early as the turn of the century. My mother, raised in Nashville, had attended Fisk's prep school as a young child. My maternal grandparents had met at Nashville's Walden College in the late 1800s. I had no idea, however, that I would be attending Fisk University until a month before it happened.

The distance between my parents' Nashville experience and mine was great. They had both moved north by the 1920s and Fisk was in the distant past. Fisk was not a household word. I can contrast this to my own children's experience. Having Fiskite parents who married two months after graduation from Fisk, my children's experience of Fisk was immediate and constant. Our best friends and their uncles and aunts were Fiskites. My husband was on the board of trustees at Fisk and Fisk stories, past and present, were prevalent in our household. This was not the case for me and my younger brother, who also went to Fisk.

I was born and raised in Illinois, spent time with relatives in Indiana and Minnesota, grandparents in Iowa, and summers in Michigan—a true Midwesterner. So, when I accompanied my parents to a medical convention at Meharry Medical School in the summer of 1953, I was visiting my mother's birth state and the Fisk University campus for the first time. It was also my first trip south. I had heard awful stories about "Jim Crow" and racial prejudice in the South, stories that had given rise to my parents' moving north. I was prepared to dislike the whole scene.

I was immediately taken aback, however, by the beauty and the southern gentility of the university campus. The manicured quadrangle, the magnolia grove, Jubilee Hall, the Chapel, the Library, all monuments to Black culture. The campus abounded with culture and class: Art, The Carl Van Vechten art collection, classical music, poetry, the spirituals of the Jubilee Singers; the presence of such renowned figures as Charles Johnson, Robert Hayden, Arna Bontemps, Aaron D. Douglass. What really overwhelmed me was to see all those beautiful Black intellectuals in one place. I am reminded of a similar statement made by W.E.B. DuBois when he first laid eyes on the campus. In Evanston, Illinois, I had often been the only Black person in my class. I have class pictures where I stick out like a sore thumb among the Olsens, Carlsens, Nielsens and the like. I had never felt at home (even "in my skin"). At Fisk, I felt at home.

My mother had known Fisk President Charles Johnson and Mrs. Johnson from their years in Chicago and in renewing acquaintances the Johnsons mentioned the Ford Foundation's Early Entrant Program and suggested that it might be something I could become a part of. They said it was rather late to take the examination, but since I was there on the campus, it could be done. They arranged for us to meet three of the Nashville students who had been accepted for the program in September, before making up my mind. I met Jane Fort, Donnetta Crippens and Jacqui McNeil. I liked them immediately. I took the examination and passed.

I was sixteen and had just finished my sophomore year at a high school that was considered one of the top-three high schools in the nation, Evanston Township High School. Graduates in the upper-tenth percentage of the high school were assured a place in any university they desired. I had already picked Wellesley or Barnard and was assured by the principal of the school that I would have no problem getting in.

The idea of my going south did not appeal to my parents. My father was afraid that a southern school could not satisfy my intellectual curiosity or, at that time, prepare me for the demands of the northern professional and business world. My mother was nervous about the racial situation in the south and afraid that my strong feelings about "Jim Crow" would "get me into trouble." I had refused to stand for, or sing, the National Anthem at school because it had "land of the free," or to say the Pledge of Allegiance because it said "liberty and justice for all" and I knew that not to be true. I had often voiced my resolve to leave the country as soon as I was able. I could not envision a minority of 12 million people forcing a nation of 20 million to change its evil ways. Better to go help a Black majority take reign, I thought. It was interesting that I missed the civil rights demonstrations by only a couple of years. I will say a little more about that later. My father was an emigrant from the British Virgin Islands. The first Black physician in the wealthy Chicago suburb of Evanston, who had given up his home to provide a hospital to save Black folks who were denied room in the local White hospital. He still believed, however, that America was the best of all possible places.

When The Ford Foundation informed us that I had qualified for the program and that the University of Chicago also had an Early Entrant

Program, the very possibility of my staying close to home gave some urgency to my determination to go to Fisk. Going to high school was my first personal experience with racial prejudice. My first years of elementary school and my junior high days were ones where Black and White students mixed freely at school, went to each other's birthday parties, met at the movies and spent hours talking on the phone. When I reached high school, however, all that changed. The Black kids, who lived in the same neighborhood as the school, walked home separately and had separate parties. I noticed in dance class during gym period the teacher would pair us up by race, and when I tried out for a school play, they cast me in the part of a maid. I had played leading roles in junior high school and in the Children's Theatre productions and I could not understand, at first, what was happening. At the reality of the racial divide, my enthusiasm about school died. The racial stories I had heard from the old south became present-day reality and I was anxious to leave. My parents gave in.

My housemates at Dunn House still tease me about arriving at Fisk that September with three trunks: one full of formals. That was my mother's idea. I had very little interest in dances, or boys, for that matter. Evanston was the type of city, an elite university town, where one went to a dress shop and sat sipping tea while the salespersons paraded outfits for you. I saw those outfits on the backs of some of my Dunn House mates many days without my knowing that they had been removed from my closet. It was no big thing. It turned out that my mother had some foresight, however, because Fisk women in those days dressed in stockings and heels, even for football games. The most constant item of attire, however, was black rubber boots with heels, which I do believe every single Fisk woman owned and wore all winter long. It was said that a Fisk girl would surely die in her boots. I remember loving those boots and have never seen anyone wear anything like them since my Fisk days.

Dunn House, a rather stark red-brick, two-story building with two steps leading up to an open concrete porch, was to become home for one year to fifteen young Basic College girls. Fisk called the Early Entrant Program the Basic College. We came from Florida, Illinois, Virginia, Alabama, Texas, Tennessee, North Carolina and Georgia. Some of us were coming from our sophomore year in high school, others from the junior year. Some were fifteen years old, others sixteen. We were told that we would be placed in classes with the regular freshmen, according to the results on our placement tests. We were also told that we could not date guys over the sophomore year at Fisk. That left basically the boys from the Black high school close by, Pearl High, the freshmen and sophomore boys at Fisk and the Basic College boys. The boys' Basic College Dormitory was just down the street from us. We were told that we would have some activities together as Basic College students (such as the "Ford Theater" drama club), but we each dined in our separate dormitories.

Our house mother was a tall, no-nonsense-looking, but actually very gentle, lady, tall, thin and almost white in complexion. Her name was Holtzclaw and we called her Mother Holtz. Later some accused her of being very class conscious and having favorites, but I was not aware of any of that while in Dunn House. I felt that she was fair and treated us all equally. Her class consciousness was supposed to have been manifested in the way she distributed roommates. It was said that my roommate, Jackie Walton, and I were placed together because my father was a physician and hers a dentist. My feeling was that roommate assignments were based on where we were from (Helen and Gloria were from Florida; Jacqui, Jane and Donnetta from Nashville; Jeanne and Carol had known each other in

Alabama, Hildred and Barbara from North Carolina) and the rest of us were more or less randomly placed. The real rationale behind selecting roommates will lie in the grave with Mother Holtz, who passed some years ago. Friendships developed as friendships do, from some indescribable spiritual connection and Jeanne Johns, Carol Pindle and I became inseparable. Some professors had difficulty distinguishing between Penn and Pindle, although in many ways we were quite different.

One of the blessings of Dunn House was Louis, an older B.C. student, who paid for part of his tuition by helping Mother Hotlz in the kitchen, serving dinner and washing dishes afterwards. We all had a crush on Louis and some took it beyond the crush stage.

In my first semester at Fisk, I felt a great need to prove myself worthy of having been selected and had the constant fear that I could not measure up. I never forgot that I had not finished high school, and that, if I did not make it at Fisk, I would have no graduation diploma at all. Again, it was only later that I was informed by my classmates in Dunn House that I was considered to have had an advantage over most of them because I came from a wealthy northern high school where I had already had Latin, algebra, geometry and some trigonometry. It was true that I was placed in some of the advanced classes, but I was not aware that some of the others had not been placed in similar classes, because we all had our separate schedules.

BCs, a shortened form for Basic College Students, were looked at as whiz kids and not always welcomed by freshmen, or some instructors, in the classrooms. I remember one occasion when I performed particularly well on a math test, I was asked to demonstrate the rationale I had used on the blackboard. When I finished the instructor said, "You see, you don't have to be a BC to get this stuff." She did not know that I was a BC and I was not about to tell her. I must say that I never encountered that attitude in any other instructor and I have to point out that this particular instructor was a new member of staff. On the contrary, one of the outstanding features about my experience at Fisk was the nurturing attitude of the professors, Black and White. I regarded them all as family.

I studied so hard that first semester that Mother Holtz told my parents that she thought I should go out more often. She said that I never dated, or sat up late at night with my card-playing housemates. The truth is that very few of us dated, which is not to say that we did not talk about boys all the time. Some of the girls claimed to have had very serious relationships with boys before coming to Fisk. We believed some of them and seriously doubted others. I had dated boys whom my parents thought were safe in groups, but never had a real one-on-one romantic relationship and never had a real kiss. There was a group of boys who represented the epitome of masculine handsomeness, intelligence and prowess to us Dunn House girls. They crossed grade levels and we made up a song about them. It went something like this: "Judson, Piggy and Terry are as fine as any men could be. Metropolitan's in there too, Graystreak is as fine as a glass of sherry wine."

While the concentration on boys was somewhat of a new experience for me, I truly enjoyed the extracurricular activities that Fisk offered, like the Stagecrafters that gave an opportunity for me to further explore my acting abilities without the concern over racism I experienced in my high school days (one of my early aspirations was to be an actress) and the Fisk University Choir, under the directorship of Von Bergen with Arthur Croley as organist. My private lessons with Professor Croley resulted in my giving an organ recital for one of the end-of-week quiet hours in the chapel. This single activity resulted in my meeting Timothy Donaldson, a fellow student and chapel deacon, who was to become my future husband, but I am getting ahead of myself. Joining the Alpha Kappa Alpha (AKA) sorority along with many of my Dunn House Girlfriends was another highlight my second year at Fisk and was something that I continued to be involved in for many years after Fisk resulting in my cofounding a chapter of the sorority (Eta Psi Omega) in the Bahamas many years later.

My grades that first semester exceeded my expectations and so I came back from Christmas vacation feeling a little more relaxed. That's when I met Metropolitan of song. He had come to visit one of my Dunn House friends and we talked. It turned out that he was in my Spanish class and, although I thought he was doing very well in the class, he said he could use some help from me. I had taken Latin in high school and had learned a lot of Spanish from my father who was from the British Virgin Islands and had spoken Spanish as a child with his relatives in Puerto Rico. Spanish came natural to me. Metropolitan and I would meet in the library and sometimes go to the coop (the favorite campus afterhours hangout) for a soda and dance afterwards. We soon became an item and were inseparable for the next two years. I had landed one of the dream boys without even trying. Mother Holtz never complained that I was neglecting my social life after that.

Metropolitan lived in Chicago, and I was just a suburb away, so our connection became year 'round and he and his whole family became very much a part of my family. When he would come to visit me in Evanston during the summer vacations, my father would keep his eye on his watch to make sure that Metropolitan did not miss the last "El" back to Chicago. When I had my debutante party at a north shore country club in the summer of 1955, Metropolitan was my escort and many of my Dunn House friends, Jeanne, Jacqui and Jane, were my attendants. Fisk friends would often accompany my family to our summer home in Idlewild,

Michigan, during the summer vacations. Gloria and Jeanne were in my wedding and Jane became the Godmother of my second son. Relationships formed at Fisk lasted throughout the years and continue to this day. Richard Ralston was one of my Basic College friends with whom I speak often even to this day some 60 years later. Richard had such a great sense of humor and because my initials were DRP, he decided to call me Inez, so that my initials would be DRIP. Richard and I cochaired our senior class program at graduation in 1958.

During the leadership retreat preceding my third year at Fisk, Timothy Donaldson whom I mentioned earlier and I started a relationship. Although my first boyfriend, Elroy Bond, was a wonderful person, I knew I was too young to think in terms of a committed relationship (about 18 then) and suggested we date other people. I had no idea that my second boyfriend, Timothy Donaldson, would end up being my husband. He was two years ahead of me, a very serious campus leader, who was also a deacon in the Chapel, as I mentioned earlier, and from the Bahamas. That courtship lasted for three years and survived a one-year separation when he went to graduate school in Minnesota. I was on exchange from Fisk in California at Pomona College and he was at the University of Minnesota. We exchanged photographs, he in earmuffs and fur-lined mittens, I in a bare-backed dress with no shoes (Pomona had quite a different dress code from Fisk). The following year we both returned to Fisk, I, to finish my senior year, and he, to teach in the mathematics department.

The experiences we both had in the new university environments were very different from the Fisk experience and served to deepen the significance of our Fisk experience. The nurturing, warm personal interactions on those campuses were limited to a few cultivated friendships, not a whole campus experience. At Fisk, with only about 500 students at that time, everyone spoke to everyone else when passing them on campus and everyone knew almost everyone by name. I had no idea who the president of Pomona was, while at Fisk I knew and admired our president, Charles S. Johnson. I found it strange on the Pomona campus to pass someone and not to speak. One of the professors at Pomona never called me anything but "the girl from Fisk." He did everything to test my mettle, giving me noticeably more difficult assignments than others and, in the end, writing a note on the postcard informing me of my final grade, to the effect that he was sorry for having underestimated me. Again, I must say that in general I was treated with every kindness at Pomona and managed to maintain my grade point average which, I was to learn later, qualified me for acceptance into Phi Beta Kappa. Social life at Pomona was quite different as well. There were no restrictions about riding in cars (girls could not do this at Fisk). Boys could see girls in their rooms for certain hours and one could stay out of the dormitory all night, if desired. The only condition was to inform the supervisor before ten o'clock so the front door could be locked. At Fisk, girls had to be in their dormitories by 10:00 P.M., without exception, and there was no question that boys were not allowed in girls' bedrooms.

Having the experience of another university campus, one highly respected, made me realize how nurturing Fisk was on a personal level, while easily measuring up academically, as well.

Being accepted in Phi Beta Kappa upon my graduation in 1958 was a highlight in my Fisk experience, not only because it was completely unexpected, but because the year I was admitted W.E.B. DuBois, the great Black activist and Fisk's most illustrious alumnus, was also accepted into the chapter. A photograph of me sitting next to him on the occasion was published in 1978 by his wife, Shirley Graham DuBois, in *DuBois: A*

Pictorial Biography. I remember discussing the trilogy he was working on at the time with him. He died shortly after that.

My fear of not measuring up at Fisk and possibly not obtaining any school diploma proved unfounded when I graduated magna cum laude, with honors in various subjects and a listing in Who's Who in American Colleges and Universities. I received a fellowship to pursue my major, Modern Foreign Languages, in a graduate school recommended by my major professor, but knew before graduation day that I would be marrying and leaving the United States, as I had promised myself many years previously.

I married Timothy Baswell Donaldson, my Fisk boyfriend, in August after my graduation, and we went to teach at a boarding school in the mountains of Kingston, Jamaica. We made wonderful friends there, isolated in a bush town, we depended on one another for work and social life. The other teachers were from all over the world, as well as Jamaica. Timothy's intention was to go to medical school at the university there, but he changed his mind and we decided to return to the United States after two years, so that he could attend law school in Chicago. Since we decided to return to my old hometown, Evanston, Illinois, and room with my parents, I applied and was accepted at Northwestern University in a special program that granted a Master's Degree in Spanish and a teaching certificate at the same time. The idea was that I would teach, but only until he finished law school.

I found that my Fisk education had prepared me well for graduate school and I finished with honors and was initiated into Pi Lambda Theta, a honorary fraternity for women in education. (It was called a fraternity and not a sorority.)

One of my professors from Northwestern University, a southern White man named Collins, chided me for an angry paper I had written based on a James Baldwin article in Harper's where I had suggested that all White people were prejudiced. He said to me, "Because you hear me speak with a southern accent, you assume that I am prejudiced, that is a prejudice you have." I realized that he was right and we became good friends. I realized much later that he was quite prominent in the field. He encouraged me to apply to be the first Negro teacher at Evanston Township High School (ETHS), my old high school. ETHS had a Black male coach, but no woman and no one in a strictly academic position. Professor Collins' daughter was one of my favorite students at ETHS. Her getting into one of my classes, I am sure, was not an accident.

My days at ETHS were short because my husband decided he was dropping out of law school and going back to the Bahamas to start a Baptist high school, at the request of his father, a Baptist bishop, and because I discovered that I was then expecting our first child, my son Dwight. After teaching one semester, I followed my husband to the Bahamas where I lived for the next 28 years, despite our initial agreement to stay there no more than five years.

I initially taught in the school my husband started for the Baptists, Prince Williams High School. Most private high schools there were run by religious denominations. My father-in-law was a Baptist bishop and the Baptists felt the need to have a Baptist school. After a few years, my husband moved on to a position in the Ministry of Education (The Government Education Department) and I was invited to be the first female teacher at Saint Augustine's High School, a Catholic high school for boys run by the Benedictine monks. I had met the dynamic, feisty headmaster at a social occasion and he discovered that I taught Spanish. He called me late one night to ask how I would like to teach at St. Augustine's College. I was surprised, but interested at the same time. I've always liked doing the unusual and this was going to be unusual—exciting and a little scary being the only woman teaching in a monastery. He teased that I was going to civilize the boys. It turned out not to be far from true. In the end, the boys were wonderful, but not before putting me to the test a few times. To this day, some 50 years later, one of my students texts me "have a blessed morning" every day.

When I look back on my years in the Bahamas, I realize the truth in the statement that time flies when you are having fun. I think I was having fun in some way, although I was never completely satisfied that I was following my own star. As the second year at St. Augustine's grew to an end, I discovered that my feelings of exhaustion and despair might be attributable to the fact that I was expecting my second son. I did not return to school in September and Kevin was born on Christmas Eve, unaided by anesthesia or any medical preparation. My husband had paged my doctor who was attending a Christmas party and grabbed a nurse about to leave the hospital.

I cannot say for certain that it was Fisk that first instilled in me the thirst for knowledge and the need to make a contribution, but I do know that it nurtured it. Having a background in music (learning the piano at age four and organ at ten), I decided to volunteer to form choirs for the boys labelled "delinquent" at the Boys Industrial School, and for able patients at Sandilands Mental Hospital (as it was called then). Both experiences gave me much joy and seemed to help enrich the lives of those involved.

After the birth of Kevin, I felt the need to do something different from teaching. I met with the Bahamas Civil Service Commission and expressed the importance of having a guidance and counseling program for the school system, as all students pursuing higher education had to navigate their way to either Canada, the U.S. or England, with very little directions to follow. I was employed to start that program and worked as an education officer in the Bahamas Ministry of Education for two years, seeing the program well launched with several teachers off to the United States to pursue degrees in Guidance and Counseling. The learning bug stung me again. While, as I said, there were no institutes of higher education in the Bahamas, there were at least two professional areas in which one could qualify locally: law and architecture. Both of them appealed to me. I had two sons in school and a husband in a demanding position in the government's Monetary Authority; leaving the island was not an option. I entered a law firm to become an articled clerk in 1970 and qualified to practice law in 1974. A fellow American female and I were cited in a local newspaper as having received the highest marks ever attained on the Bahamas Bar Examinations, a feat I attribute to my Fisk heritage, where Dr. Johnson urged us to be the best we could be. For the next ten years, I was very active in the Bahamas Bar Association, chaired various committees and served as its secretary and vice president. I taught law for the University of the West Indies' Degree Program in Hotel Management and Tourism, helped to initiate a legal aid clinic and spent a short stint as a magistrate in the lower court. Being on the board of Crossroads, an organization concerned with the care of the homeless, offered me an opportunity to attend a church service one Sunday, led by the leader of Crossroads, the Rev. Hesketh Johnson, who announced the need for housing a homeless young girl from the mentally retarded school whose only caregiver, her grandmother, had died. I immediately thought of my large home, with two sons away in school, and offered to provide a home for the girl. Angela lived with my husband and me until her marriage a few years later.

My life in the Bahamas was exciting. My husband held a public office as Governor of the Central Bank and I had met many dignitaries and celebrities—been entertained by Queen Elizabeth, dined with Prince Charles, met President Nixon, became friends with Sidney Poitier and so forth. I had help at home, maids, gardeners and chauffeurs. Lived an upper-middle-class life with every material possession I could even dream of. At age forty, however, I discovered that the midlife crisis was real, not the fiction I had assumed it to be. I looked back over my life and asked myself if I wanted to spend the rest of my life this way. The uncertain answer was, no. I had been married over twenty years, my children were away in school, both in the United States, and I felt I had never really been an autonomous person—mapping my own way rather than that determined by my husband and circumstances. I had reached an unhappy impasse in my life.

I left the law firm, in which I was a partner, took some courses in Los Angeles, where my mother lived, first at UCLA in public relations and screenplay courses, then received a certificate in interior design at an Interior Design school in Beverly Hills. Returning to Nassau, I did some public relations work for my church and took on a major interior design job for ten doctors who were starting a joint practice. (I had represented the Doctor's Union when I was practicing law.) I realized that I was just dabbling, however, and still felt a sense of not knowing what I wanted to do with the rest of my life.

As fate would have it, the Universe made a decision for me. There were two determining factors. As I was driving home from having visited a car dealership one sunny afternoon, I encountered a car blocking the narrow road and the driver getting out of the car. I stopped and walked toward him to ask if I could help. When I asked if he was all right, he put a gun in my face, knocked me to the ground and took off with my car. He later was shot down by the police, but not until he had harmed many others. I was the only one spared and my story of the incident was published in a

New Thought publication which was entitled "Sorry, but I was Held-up," demonstrating the double entendre of an expression I made to the dealer who later called to ask why I had not followed up on the possible purchase from him. This created a fear in me never experienced before in the island.

The second incident that ultimately gave rise to my leaving the island occurred after a hard day of attempting to rise to occasions. It was a Friday, end of the week, and I had a luncheon party at my home for the wife of the American ambassador that exceeded the time period that I had allotted for the occasion. I had assumed that after a couple of hours the lunch would have ended and I would be able to meet the workmen before closing time at the site where I was directing the interior design for the ten doctors mentioned earlier. The luncheon ladies were enjoying themselves so much, however, that it became clear that they had no intention of leaving and so I, very apologetically, had to ask their forgiveness for leaving to meet my obligation at the decorating site. I invited them to stay on, which was rather awkward, but my housekeeper was there to attend to their needs. I barely made it to the decorating site in time to pay the workers, after which I had arranged to stop by my church to give the minister a copy of an article I had written for the Sunday bulletin. When I presented it to him and he suggested some changes, he later told me the look on my face betrayed a kind of disappointment or despair he had never seen on my face before. I made the changes and left his office to return home to a telephone message from a good friend asking if I could fill in for a missing bridge partner at her home that evening. She sounded desperate and so I agreed. The bridge party ended after midnight and I drove home, nearby, and awakened my husband with the news that I was home and not feeling so good.

The pain in my stomach rapidly increased and after trying several homemade remedies, it became clear that professional help was needed.

The bridge card friend was a medical doctor whom we knew was still awake at that hour, so he called her first. She brought medication that didn't work, and so another friend, a surgeon, was called. He arrived as soon as possible with medication that also did not work, and so my general practitioner was called. He came to the house with medication that did not work. My obstetrician who lived nearby was then called. He came as well and after examining me said that it was not a problem, he could address and with four doctors present it was decided that I needed to be hospitalized as soon as possible. Another medical friend was called and asked to apprise the hospital that I was on my way for immediate admittance. The diagnosis was pancreatitis and after a two-week stay in Princess Margaret Hospital in Nassau, I was air-ambulanced to a hospital in Miami. Two weeks later, I was released from the hospital, but urged to stay nearby in the case of the relapse. My husband and I had acquired a second home in Washington, D.C., where a Fisk friend was a chief surgeon at Howard University's hospital, so that seemed to be the logical place to go. The move to that house marked the end of my life in the Bahamas. After thirty-one years of marriage, my husband, Timothy, and I divorced and I moved to the United States permanently.

By this time my two sons were living in the States and making marks for themselves. In many ways, they exemplified the spirit that Fisk had instilled in their parents to make a contribution to society. David, who had first thought acting was his goal and had matriculated at the prestigious Julliard School, after attending the equally prestigious Wesleyan University decided to go on to New York University and pursue a career in psychiatric social work as well as a career in writing and becoming a published author, and Kevin, following his parents' love of music, wrote and produced his own music, and also worked as a costume designer for film and fashion specialists.

Anthropology had always been a subject that I found attractive. The fact that my father was a West Indian may have been a factor. From early childhood, I had been interested in foreign places, diverse peoples and ways of life. My mother said she always knew that I would marry a foreigner. In seeking a new direction in my life, anthropology loomed high. I thought of combining it with law and doing the subfield of legal anthropology. So I applied for a course called "An Introduction to the U.S. Legal System" at Georgetown University in Washington. One thought was to get a master's degree in Law and pursue teaching. My second thought was to get a Ph.D. in Anthropology and write.

Again, calling on my Fisk connections, I called my Dunn House mate, Gloria Marshall, who had gained a name for herself in the field of anthropology under the name Niara Sudarkasa, and told her I was thinking of studying anthropology, because I needed credibility for my newly anticipated writing career. "You don't need a degree in Anthropology for that," she assured me. Well, that did not daunt me, and at age fifty I entered the graduate school at The American University in Washington to pursue a doctorate in Anthropology. It took me seven years, with coursework, field work, writing a 400-plus-page dissertation, divorcing, remarrying and moving to an island on the Chesapeake Bay, to complete the process.
In 1992, I married James Towns, a Washington dentist from Oklahoma who had attended the University of Iowa and Howard University's Dental School. We had the Midwestern and the Historically Black College experiences in common. A widower, his three grown children became an added asset to my family.

Working on the dissertation for my doctorate afforded me an opportunity to delve further into the issue that had caused me to leave the United States almost thirty years earlier. That issue was racism. I chose to look into how racism affected the education of minorities and in particular that of young Black males. The year-long research resulted in my dissertation entitled "The Impact of Structural Hypocrisy on the School Performance of Young African-American Males" (1996).

The publication of this dissertation got the attention of Dr. Wade Boykins, a psychology professor at Howard University, who was heading a federally funded research project there called the Center for Research on the Education of Students Placed at Risk (CRESPAR). I was hired as the anthropologist on a multi-disciplinary team of educators, sociologists and psychologists.

My goal of going into anthropology in order to publish was realized sooner than I had expected as a few of my works were published: "Rewind the World: An Ethnographic Study of Inner-City African-American Children's Perceptions of Violence" (1996); "Successes and Challenges in Triangulating Methodologies in Evaluations of Exemplary Urban Schools" (2004); "The Journey to Urban School Success: Going the Extra Mile" (2001) and others that were coauthored with colleagues in the project.

Reinforcing my Fisk connections, when I moved to the Washington area, I reunited with many of my old Fisk friends, including six of the Dunn House girls: Jeanne Johns Adkins, Maryann Gay Rozzell, Carol Pindle Smith, Hildred Roach Stafford, Niara Sudarkasa (the Basic College gang paid a tribute to her at her inauguration as the first female president of the historical Lincoln University) and Jackie Walton Sadler, my first roommate. It was Jackie, working for the D.C. Public School System at the time, who made the initial entrée that enabled me to do my dissertation research in the public school system in the District of Columbia. After completing the five-year Howard University project, I initially rejected the idea of retirement, although I had reached an acceptable age and calling upon my legal training, I took up the position of legislative aide to a Maryland State Senator. After a couple of years with Senator Teitelbaum, who was contemplating retirement himself, I decided to retire and to move to Florida, where the aged go for the last hoorah.

In retirement, the concept of "giving back" loomed high and I sought ways in which I could do just that. Working with illiterate adults for the Palm Beach Library Literacy program proved to be as rewarding to myself as I hope it was to those I mentored. Having a background in anthropology, and a great deal of cross-cultural experience, I was able to assist other literacy instructors by lecturing from time to time on cross-cultural issues that might affect literacy teaching. Mentoring homeless women at the Lord's Place and handing out food to the homeless on behalf of Unity Church through CROS Ministries have helped to fulfill my life in retirement and hopefully to satisfy my mission on this earth.

At the age of 84, looking back on my life, I can unequivocally say that my days at Fisk shaped my life in so many ways; I cannot articulate them all. Most obvious were the relationships: my marriage to a Fiskite, my youngest brother, his wife and son being Fiskites and my deepest sustaining friendships. Also, however, were the more subtle aspects of instilling in me the love and thirst for knowledge, the belief in the contribution that African-Americans have made and continue to make to the country and the world, and President Charles Johnson's pricking of my conscience to go out and make the world a better place.

Then

Now

Donna, Received Ph.D. in Anthropology from the American University, 1995

Donna, called to the Bahamas Bar, 1974

Dunn House Girls' Reunion 2000. Kent Island, Maryland
Standing Left to Right: Carole Pindle, Jackie Walton, Jane Fort, Hildred Roach, Barbara Crockett. Maryann Gay, Jeanne Johns
Seated Left to Right: Donna Penn, Gloria Marshall

Cotillion: Donna & parents

Jane, Jacqui, Donna and Jeanne

Maryann Rebecca Gay Rozzell

Prologue

The bonds that began in the fall of 1953 with our year at Dunn House as young teens admitted to Fisk University without the usual completion of high school studies have continued strong. As I planned how to share the story of my life experiences, I saw the reach of Fisk as it extended to generations before me so this is where I begin my story.

My maternal great-grandfather was Benjamin Johnson (1808-1896) of Edgecombe County, North Carolina. He and Rebecca Norris (1818-1906) were married in 1845 and I know they were free people because their marriage bonds were posted in county records as was not allowed for the enslaved. On the farm they owned in Lower Fishing Creek Township they raised seven children. One of their daughters was Martha (1855-1932).

Also in Edgecombe County, Lewis, a blacksmith, born in 1826, and Lizzie Newsome Bullock, born 1833, were raising a family of seven children. Lewis and Lizzie are signed in the Freedmen's Cohabitation Records of 1866 as having been living as man and wife for 16 years, "having been lately slaves."Their son, George (1855-1943), married Martha Johnson on Christmas Eve 1879.

The first child of George and Martha was George Lewis Bullock (1885-1968). My mother, Lula Rebecca Bullock (1895-1967), was the sixth of their children. Because she will be often mentioned, I introduce Jessie Lea (1900-1998), who was seventh and lastborn child of this family group.

A young man of mixed racial parentage, Thomas Sewell Inborden (1865-1925) left Upperville, his home in the foothills of Virginia, to seek work and education in Oberlin, Ohio. Following some study there, he found his way to Fisk University where he graduated in 1890. After having worked as an educator at several schools that were under the auspices of the American Missionary Association (AMA), as was Fisk, Mr. Inborden was asked to take on the task of establishing a school on a former plantation in Edgecombe County, North Carolina. Mrs. Julia Brick, a wealthy White New York widow, had given the land for this school to the AMA. It was to be named the Joseph Keasby Brick School and the AMA was contributing to its support and organization. The founding date was 1895.

George and Martha Bullock were among those invited to bring their family to live as tenants in one of the homes on the spacious grounds of the Brick School. They wisely realized the advantages of having education for their children so close to a home that included land for farming. Far better than the sharecropping which they had been struggling with for several years. The cost of schooling for the children was 50 cents, paid twice per school year, for each child! The Bullocks lived on the Brick campus for 15 years and all seven offspring did farm labor, going out to work the fields after classes and getting their studying done after darkness fell.

By 1909, oldest son George Lewis Bullock, having finished the course of study at Brick School, went off to Nashville to attend Fisk University.

After two years of study there, he went to teach at Strait School, which later became Dillard University, in New Orleans. Sister Lula followed his path to Nashville and in 1917 graduated from Fisk and began her teaching career in Covington, Kentucky.

Courtship and Family

Wolsey Gay was a young teen seeking an education. At his home in rural Dodge County, Georgia, he heard news of a school not far away in Talladega, Alabama, which had been established in 1869 with the combined support of the American Missionary Association and the Freedmen's Bureau. He set out to attend this school despite mild parental objections. As he told me the story, his dad told him he would be treated badly there "because he was a poor boy."

Undeterred, Wolsey enrolled in Talladega where he learned the trade of barbering, was treasurer of his class, and graduated from the college in 1918. Having experienced the AMA-related school setting, it is not surprising that Wolsey Gay made his way to eastern North Carolina to teach in the science department of the Brick School and once established there became assistant to the principal, T. S. Inborden.

Not insignificant is the fact that while there he became acquainted with the Bullock family, including daughter Lula, who was teaching high school students in Covington, Kentucky.

She often made visits home to see her parents and on 1 July 1922 Lula and Wolsey were in Salisbury, N.C., at the home of Pearl, Lula's older sister, whose husband, the Reverend Ananias Croom, joined the two in matrimony.

On his twenty-fifth birthday, 18 August 1923, Wolsey became the father of Wolsey Gay Junior. I imagine how delighted George and Martha were to have the young couple living in their home with the additional joy of a baby grandson. However, an offer came to Wolsey to head a newly built seventeen-teacher Rosenwald school in the not-too-distant town of Dunn, North Carolina. The move was made. The Harnett County Training School was one of the almost 5000 Rosenwald-funded schools built between 1920 and 1932. The building still stands and in 2014 was placed on the National Register of Historic Places.

Moving Once More

By 1930 a request came from Alabama and Wolsey, Lula and Jr. moved to Talladega. Wolsey took the job as director of the practice schools operated by Talladega College. Sessions was the elementary school, and the secondary school where he was the principal was called Drewry. Both provided students of the college with supervised teaching opportunities in a setting providing education to Black students on a level far better than that provided in the public schools of Alabama in those days of segregation. Actually, the Talladega public system did not provide Black students with education beyond eighth grade in the years before 1948.

A traumatic event befell the family in 1932, not long after their relocation. On a visit to Lula's brother, George, who lived in Louisville, Kentucky, Junior became ill. He complained of a headache, was taken to a hospital and by the end of the day had died of scarlet fever. He was nine years, 20 days old, and the reverberations of his loss have never ceased.

I Enter the Scene

On 9 November 1937 my family home on Rangeline Road, Talladega, Alabama, was on fire. I had been born on the seventh and my dad, Wolsey Gay, had built up fire in the furnace to get the house warmed up for bringing my mother, Lula, and me home from the hospital. His prediction, shortly after the fire, which was only a few sparks igniting some roof shingles, was that I would grow up to marry a fireman. I never, ever considered it!

We moved to another home shortly before my fourth birthday. I remember being intrigued by the stairs there and that I enjoyed lying horizontally on the top stair and rolling to the bottom stair. Another thing that fascinated me about that house was that the prior occupants, the Kindles, had moved to Maryland. Somewhere, I had heard stories about druids and Mr. Kindle, a physical education teacher when at Talladega, was to be in charge of the Druid Hill YMCA in Baltimore. You can't imagine my thoughts about the wild adventures the Kindles would have with druids in that Maryland city!! (I have always had a vivid imagination as will be a continuing theme in my story.)

Both of these homes were on the campus of Talladega College. Talladega College had from its beginnings a racially mixed community, faculty, staff and students. The system of laboratory schools, known as "practice schools," was the only possible way for the children of Talladega's White faculty and staff members to be adequately educated in Talladega. Their lives would have been unbearable had they attempted to attend the town's White schools because they were "tainted" by association with people of color.

I entered Sessions Elementary School, two months before my fifth birthday. My teacher was Mae E. Addison, a single lady from the Chicago area. She looked somewhat like a 1940s version of Elizabeth Warren. The kindergarten classroom had a housekeeping area with dolls and cradles, a basket of dress-up clothes, a reading corner with shelves of books, a comfy rug for sitting to read and a block building and wooden train area. Clay, crayons, paper, scissors and glue were in the art area along with an easel holding a pad of newsprint. We kids quickly discovered that the chalky blackboard erasers could be used for making mischief.

A piano stood at the far end of the room and our choral repertoire included "Down by the Station," "The More We Get Together" and nursery tunes. There are now books written on the premise of "all that I ever needed to know I learned in kindergarten." As I remember Miss Addison's kindergarten and the class gathered around her for the song with which we ended every day, I find there is truth in this. My grandson Nick wrote this music out for me in January 2020. A philosophy for life is in its lyric "Be always kind and true."

The school playground had a paved sidewalk along the length of the building which was great for many activities. We brought chalk out of the classroom for drawing hopscotch. Kids had metal roller skates with ball bearings and a key was needed to adjust the clamps that gripped the front part of your shoe. Skates were fun to use on the sidewalks. My first-grade teacher distinguished herself on the playground by being able to roller skate backward. Miss Jordan was also an enthusiastic and dedicated teacher. The day that I was able to read cover to cover the Dick and Jane first-grade reader, she walked with me to my house after school so that I could read the book to my mother.

Miss Jordan had come from New York to teach and the ways of the South presented her with a different experience than she had as a young Black woman growing up north of the Mason-Dixon Line. Bernice Jordan met a Tuskegee Airman, Dudley Malone Watson. They fell in love and decided to marry in June of 1943. The reality of the deep south was that there was no place within many miles of Talladega or Tuskegee where they could have a comfortable honeymoon. My parents offered them space and meals at our home. Unfortunately, I thought my teacher was there to visit me and still remember my mother tugging me by the sash of my dress to get me to go out in the yard or elsewhere to play so the newlyweds could have some time undisturbed.

My education progressed uneventfully through the next several years. Carolyn Terrell was a classmate and good friend with whom I sometimes traded the sandwich I had brought to school for lunch. I enjoyed her sandwiches which she said were tripe. In conversation with my mother, I revealed my new lunch menu and she then told me that tripe was the stomach of a cow. After that I ate the lunches prepared for me!

Carolyn walked to school across the town of Talladega from a community called McCannville with her two younger sisters. Her start in school was delayed a year because at six her mother considered her too young to walk all the way through the downtown area safely. Busses for school kids were unheard of at that time, in that place. My other good friend, Erma Ruth Adams, was one of five children in her immediate family and she had a cousin, Lillian Marie, who also attended our school. I felt very isolated as one of the only people, it seemed to me, to not have relatives at our school to "stand up for me." A really sore point with me was that a few of my classmates were uncles or aunts to other kids close to our age. My cousins were all much older and they and my aunts and uncles lived a great distance away.

I knew that I once had a brother though minimal information was given to me by parents or others about his life and death. If I asked either parent about him, I was told, "We don't want to talk about that because it would make your mother/father sad." I had my own ideas about the situation related to my interpretation of church activities I had observed. I had been informed that the money collected in the offerings during church service was "for God." My theory was that the money was transmitted to God by burning. I had not been in a church where there were censers but the upward wafting of smoke is, I suppose, why I pictured this. In order to make contact with my late brother, my scheme was to send him "mail" by smoke. I wrote many letters and pleas to him along with prayers to God for some contact or information as to his wellbeing and current activities. There was a concrete driveway bridge under which I placed my burning pleas as I was at least mindful of the danger of fires. As high school principal, my father had in his desk drawer at work many items he confiscated from "wayward" students, including matchbooks. When unobserved, I grabbed those and other items about which I had no inkling of their use. This would include condoms.

Also, I felt responsible for my parents' reputation as I overheard family and friends say, "Lula and Wolsey are going to spoil that child to death!" I was as undemanding as I could be (in my mind) in that effort.

I desperately wanted a sibling and made prayerful bargains with God that I would care for my doll, Carol, as if she were a live baby, feeding, diaper changes, etc., for a whole week to prove what a good sister I would be if my parents would have another child! After a visit to the home of my great uncle I picked out a little girl that I wanted to adopt as my sister. There were many children and grandchildren there and I thought one could be spared to live with us!

My household pet was a black-and-white cat named Bucky. We never had a dog but my parents' friend, Ethel Miller, known to me as Aunt Ethel, had a German shepherd dog named Carl. We had a chicken coop at the far end of our yard where we kept white leghorn hens to provide us with eggs. Also in that henhouse lived a fluffy Rhode Island Red chicken whose name was Judy. She was my pet. One balmy afternoon I had let Judy out in the yard to play. Aunt Ethel and my mother were chatting as they sat on the back steps and Carl, the dog, was sniffing around the yard. Suddenly Judy caught Carl's attention and before we could react, he chased her into a bed of iris and had her in his jaws. Aunt Ethel, a nurse, asked for a paper bag, put Judy in the bag and went home. My mom said that Judy might be healed since Aunt Ethel was a nurse but I knew that would not happen. I was devastated.

My mother belonged to a women's group, the Dunbar Relief Club. They provided food baskets, clothing and other charitable aid to community families. Word came to the group that a child had eaten from a garbage can outside of the college dining hall where food was discarded. This little girl had developed food poisoning and died. The Dunbar Relief Club women took the responsibility for assisting the family with the costs of a respectful burial. My mother had a "parenting encyclopedia" that I surreptitiously read as much as she did. It presented the idea that to help a child accept death with lessened trauma it was helpful to let them have experience with a death that was not that of a close family member. My mother took on the job of shopping for a dress for the child to be buried in and accordingly took me to view her in the casket when all was ready. The dress was white and its blue sash had been cut into two ribbons for her braids. This experience and my family's continual service to those in their communities made a deep impression on me with regard to helping others.

My father spent much non-school time interacting with the families of his students to encourage parental support of regular attendance at school and good academic achievement. In addition, he was a founder and active member of the Men's Civic League. Access to voting was an issue demanding attention as there were ongoing efforts by area Whites to limit the number of voters from the Black and general college connected community. The league worked diligently to improve access to the polls and informed voting.

Dad was very much a radio fan and had two favorite programs. One was the broadcasts of the vocal group Wings Over Jordan. A song he really loved was "Deep River." I was often in trouble over his other favorite, H. V. Kaltenborn, the newscaster. The required silence during that broadcast was hard for me to maintain!!

I too had a favorite radio program and it came on Saturday morning. It was "Let's Pretend," sponsored by Cream of Wheat and timed to conflict with the swim class for faculty children. My mother was all too familiar with stories of kids getting drowned in creeks and quarries that had no lifeguards and was insistent that I take the class instead of listening to the radio program.

No Green Book, but We Traveled

One advantage of having teachers as my parents was that when school was out for the summer we could take family trips. The pattern of our travel was set by places and people with whom we could find safe haven. We would drive to Atlanta where my Uncle Ben lived and that was our first overnight stop. He taught agriculture at Atlanta University and was a beekeeper. I loved to chew on the wax of the honeycombs.

Next stop was Durham, N.C., at the home of my mother's elder sister, Aunt Pearl. That visit had several advantages and the first is that the across the street neighbors were the Walton family with two kids, Veora and

"Brother," who were close to my age and much fun to play with. Unfortunately, they also liked to tease me by shout-singing the song "I've come from Alabama with a banjo on my knee." They loved my unhappy reaction... but we remained friends. The other draw was that the best yeast rolls I've ever eaten were made by my cousin Dorcas who, though a teacher at Hillside High School and married, lived there in her parents' home. She also made very good cornbread.

We sometimes stopped briefly in King's Mountain on the way to Durham. That stop was fraught with stress for my mother. Her childhood friend, Mrs. Ricks, taught there at Lincoln Academy but the source of the anxiety was the fact that the son of Mrs. Ricks had polio.

I had marching orders to touch as little as possible, keep my hands away from my face and mouth, not to accept anything to eat or drink and as soon as the visit ended and we returned to the car I was thoroughly wiped down with a washcloth. Lest I forget, one of the places we passed on this leg of the trip was Crowders Mountain, where Mom provided me with a history lesson as she often did in our travels.

We made a stop at the home of friends in Roselle, NJ, where there was a daughter, Gene Ann, who was a physician. I was a huge fan of hers as she was the only female MD that I knew. A role model whose steps I never followed, though it was my plan for a while.

The grand finale of many of these treks was the summer home of my Uncle Joe in Oak Bluffs, Martha's Vineyard. My favorites there were the carousel at Vineyard Haven, lobster rolls, and the wild blueberries that could be picked all over the island.

Some summers, my dad taught teacher workshops in various communities. One summer that I remember well, my mom and I went with him to Valdosta, Georgia, and stayed with the family of one of the teachers.

There were two daughters near my age in the family and I was startled and impressed when we three kids were on our own at lunchtime one day and the girls cooked porkchops with rice and gravy. It had never occurred to me, though I don't remember how old I was (ten or eleven), that I could have actually cooked part of a real meal.

Entertainment for All

It was the era of Jackie Robinson and everyone we were on speaking terms with was a fan of the Brooklyn Dodgers!! At World Series time the sound of baseball broadcasts could be heard through any open window of car or house.

My parents' favorite social activity was playing bridge. I was not fond of their bridge nights when the games were at our house because I got put to bed early. But the times when they played at the home of another faculty couple, a college student came to "babysit" me and I got to stay up late. (I have never wanted to learn to play bridge, though I did play Canasta briefly when it became popular.)

In my family/friend circle there was NO attending of the Ritz Theatre downtown where Black patrons were expected to buy tickets at the box office then go down an alley to a side entrance, go upstairs and sit in the balcony. I heard from some who did ignore the taboo that there was an occasional peanut or two thrown down onto patrons below.

The college provided Friday night movies in the college chapel at the cost of a dime for kids. My parents carefully prescreened those to decide if I was allowed to attend. (I sat close to the screen with my friends, mostly other campus brats, and so had no idea that I was nearsighted for many years.) My mother was most enthusiastic about Bing Crosby, other musicals and Disney films. "Tura, Lura, Lura" runs through my head at times.

We also had the opportunity to see professional presentations brought to campus under sponsorship of New England benefactors. The Sadler's Wells Ballet Company was one that stands out in my memory. My good friend, Sandra Knox, and I stuffed tissues into the toes of our sneakers in order to dance "on point" for months after that.

Some of these programs were attended by a few of the White citizens of the town who put aside their segregationist views for the sake of a good play or musical performance. One of the attendees was a Mr. Tom Abernathy, editor of the local paper, Talladega Daily News. Now when there were certain events on the campus such as a Y.M.C.A. regional convention which drew groups of Whites and Blacks to attend, the Ku Klux Klan would appear in an early evening procession of cars driving through the campus. People in the cars were robed and hooded, shotguns and Confederate flags protruded from the windows. I never heard of any violence happening on those "parade" evenings. The intent was to cause fear and intimidation and I suppose that was achieved to some extent. Adult discussion was limited when young listeners were around. We were convinced, however, that some in the cars were those who had attended some of the college programs.

The Royal Shakespeare Company performed some plays in the chapel and we also had the college's own Little Theatre productions under the directorship of Miss Lillian Voorhees, who later was my speech teacher at Fisk. Sol Hurok Presents brought Marian Anderson in concert and we heard Langston Hughes and others speak. Of course, the college choir, under the direction of Frank Harrison was superb and one of its soloists, Carol Bryce, went on to perform as a "first" with the Houston (TX) Opera Company.

My absolute favorite event at the chapel occurred each spring. That was the Elks Oratorical Contest. I greatly enjoyed the recitations of area high school students who competed for scholarship funds. Had I been a judge I would have awarded first prize for the very dramatic rendition of "Curfew Shall Not Ring Tonight". Although my mother could, and often did, recite long poems such as "Hiawatha" and "Evangeline," the only poem I ever learned in its entirety was "The Midnight Ride of Paul Revere."

Entertainment away from home was often problematic as there were some places that had "days" for Black patrons. On a visit to my cousin, Blanche, who taught in Columbia, near Roanoke, N.C., we wanted to see the acclaimed production "Lost Colony." We learned that the only day Blacks could attend was Tuesday. For that event we did not hold to the taboo against segregated events and we enjoyed a dramatic Tuesday performance.

Religion

Many of my schoolmates were children of other Talladega faculty members.

One of my close pals was Peter Rasmussen. He and his brother David were children of one of the Jewish faculty families. Peter and I saved cereal box tops selectively and cooperatively and ordered prizes that were available for redemption. We were so enterprising as to go to the college dietician and ask her to set aside whatever empty boxes we needed for some specific prize.

I was never sure that we, the Black community, were not Jewish ourselves. The Jordan River mentioned in song and prayer was certainly not in the Deep South. "Go Down Moses" was an oft heard song. And didn't we have a history of captivity!! "Let my people go." But then we were also touched by "Danny Boy" which was rendered movingly by the high school P.E. teacher/coach. The campus community made many Jewish refugees welcome, this was the 1940s. They held positions on the faculty and staff. I heard firsthand stories of narrow escapes from S.S. troops in Germany and

Poland but had no idea what the horrors of the war and the Holocaust were in reality.

As a family, we attended the college chapel nondenominational services and sometimes went to the small Congregational Church just off campus. My parents wanted me to attend a Sunday School so arranged for me to go with my friend Erma Adams to Jacob's Chapel C.M.E. Church also just off the campus. There several of my friends and I won silver dollars for reciting Bible verses, found a discarded bottle of "white lightning" in tall grass while on our way one Sunday and had other adventures. I also sang in the youth choir. Talent was not required.

One summer I attended vacation Bible School at Mt. Canaan Baptist Church. What I remember most about that is stopping to buy tiny little wax bottles with a few drops of some sweet colored liquid as we kids left the church headed for home.

Respect and Race

New England Congregationalists showed ongoing support for the college by sending "gently used" clothing and household items to the college. At this point the college student body was not interested in or in real need of these boxes of donations. They were turned over to the Dunbar Relief Club for disbursal for the good of the community. This resulted in my mother operating a used clothing shop from our basement. Mrs. Molliston was one of the patrons of this shop I remember well. She was a White cotton mill factory worker with children and grandchildren and very little money. She shopped regularly, often bringing coworkers and always greeting my mom with a "Hello, Mrs. Gay" and announcing to others who had come with her, if it was a first time for them, that "this is Mrs. Gay." Using a title for a Black woman would have been unheard of by this group of people in this time and place but as she helped them sort through clothes looking for sizes and suitability a rapport developed between these women that possibly changed some attitudes.

My dad definitely had his commercial choices influenced by racial attitudes. The proprietor of a Texaco gas station near the campus always addressed him as "Professor." This won the loyalty of Daddy for Texaco anywhere. As we traveled, he was careful to enter a service station and before the gas was put in the car tank ask if his wife and daughter could use the restroom. If restroom use was not permitted, we drove on to the next Texaco for our fill-up!

Meanwhile: My Education

My education took a turn for the unique when the people in charge of the practice schools, either the college powers that were or the American Missionary Association, decided that the City of Talladega should be forced to do the right thing and provide full public K-12 education for its Black citizens. The plan consisted of closure of the elementary and high school laboratory schools but with a provisional school of reduced size, again because of the dilemma facing the children of the White faculty members. A school of much reduced size and comprised of three groups of students was developed. The total enrollment of this continuation school was at one time 25. That was about the average, I believe. We had three main teachers, supplemented mainly by college students majoring in education who therefore were students of my father's. He had become a full-time teacher in the college education department with the closure of the lab schools.

The education was still highly regarded and one of the teachers in a county school was eager for her daughter to attend. Arrangements were made for Mrs. Estelle to bring Carolyn to our house early each morning with her lunch and an afterschool snack. Carolyn and I walked to school together, home for lunch and back after school till she was picked up by her mom. Carolyn was fun, quiet and almost like having a little sister. One sunny morning as we neared the school building a man who had been leaning against a car across the street from the school dashed quickly forward and grabbed Carolyn by the shoulders, dragging her backward toward the car. We both screamed at the top of our lungs, I threw my armful of books at the man's head and ran into the school to the room of the one male teacher in the building, the art teacher, Claude Clarke. By the time Mr. Clarke and I exited the building two men who had been painting the exterior of a house next to the school had blocked the man from putting Carolyn into the car. The three men got Carolyn released and detained the would-be kidnapper until a policeman arrived.

I learned later that the man was Carolyn's father who had been estranged from the family but wanted to have custody of his daughter. By the end of the school year Earline and Carolyn Estelle had relocated to Indiana.

One of the teachers, Mrs. Hamilton, led us in a production of *Aïda* complete with costumes and staging. This was my eighth- or ninth-grade year and she incorporated geography and some math in the preparation for the mini-opera. Not a standard curriculum but fun.

Basically, my education was falling apart at this point because I got away with manipulating the course of study, skipping algebra because I preferred geometry, not studying because there was no one actually on my grade level to compete with and I had no self-directed push to learn.

There were two educational things I loved to do. If my mother was serving as a substitute teacher in a county school, I always read the textbooks she was using. I did not want her to teach students anything I did not know!! The subjects she usually taught were History and Latin. She sometimes worked at the community library and I loved to spend time there with her in my afterschool hours. I seriously considered becoming a librarian thinking that when I wasn't checking out books for someone or shelving them, I could read and read and read!

My parents were expressing growing concern regarding my lack of a peer group and range of educational experiences and they were considering sending me to Palmer Memorial Institute in Sedalia, N.C., but were reluctant to have me leave home. They provided me with a couple of summer camp experiences at Camp Atwater in East Brookfield, Mass. That provided great memories and peer friendships. I remember from my first camp year when my mom met my Birches Cabin counselor and found out that she, Therrel Smith, was a graduate of her beloved Fisk University, that fact wiped away the tears Mom was about to shed at bidding me goodbye!

A plan evolved to move me a grade ahead so I could attend the public school which was by now extended to include high school through grade twelve. My dad was at this time full-time professor of secondary education so he could have major input through the student teachers that were assigned to Westside High School and be reassured that the academic program was satisfactory. Thus at fourteen I began my first and only public school year entering the eleventh grade.

I already knew many of my classmates and we got along well. Two of my favorite classmates were from the State School for the Blind and Deaf. They, Emma Deyampert and Thora Dudley, had "readers" and used Braille materials to manage doing their schoolwork and they were academic high achievers. Keeping up with the academic program required little study from me and I was still not a competitive student.

I found new social experiences and different standards of behavior among some of my peers very intriguing. As an example, one girl shredded a classmate's clothes in the locker room because she thought her boyfriend responsible for the other girl's pregnancy!

A New Plan

Dr. John Morrow taught Modern Foreign Languages at Talladega College and his daughter, Jean, and I were friends. We had fun playing the duets in the *Etude Music Magazine* on the piano at her home or mine. Most of her education was in Hackensack, NJ, where the family lived previously.

Jean visited in Talladega at Christmas holidays of 1952 bubbling over with excitement about a program she was in called Basic College. When Jean's mother spoke to my mother about this program at Fisk my mother caught the excitement. After all, it was at Fisk!

The setup for the students to have dorms and house parents distinct from the standard college freshman, an academic dean for the Basic College plus financial support from the Ford Foundation was of great weight with both parents.

I haven't yet mentioned that my tenth birthday was ruined because that was the November of the inauguration of Charles S. Johnson as President of Fisk. My parents had met Dr. Johnson while doing summer studies for their Master's degrees at Columbia University and events at her alma mater always interested my mother. She went to Nashville for the inauguration and all I saw of her on that birthday was during our drive to Birmingham to put her on the train to Nashville. My present, which I opened in the car, was bunny-eared bedroom slippers.

Beginning by being a mother's helper in the homes of some faculty families/neighbors I had progressed to doing regular babysitting. One of the families I sat for was that of the Talladega College recruitment officer, Bill Twyman. When the SATs were given at Westside High School in my eleventh-grade year, Mr. Twyman was monitoring the testing. He passed close to my desk and said quietly, "I know you put Talladega as your choice of schools to get the test results." Having a maverick streak, and despite my animosity over the birthday slight, I put "Fisk."

Jean had said being in Basic College was fun!!!

Dunn House

My parents and I arrived in Nashville after many wardrobe and other consultations with Jean and Mrs. Morrow. Mother Holtz welcomed me and I was assigned to room with Ellena Stone from Houston and Eva Walker from Chicago. One of my fondest hopes for what I considered an even playing field was immediately dashed by the revelation that two of the residents, Carol and Jeanne, had known each other previously. Nonetheless it was great to have instant siblings and a "big brother," Lou Garner, who came to take care of the kitchen cleanup after our communal dinner meal.

Before my parents departed for home my mother introduced me to two longtime campus personalities, Cecile Jefferson and Mary D. Shane. I was then on my own in a new life as a college student albeit in a sheltered setting.

College Life

Not only had I never developed study habits in my variegated years of schooling, but student organizations and other such activities were unfamiliar to me. I remember when one of the Dunn House conversations was about election of officers for some group and *Robert's Rules of Order* was mentioned. I innocently chimed in, "Why does Robert get to make the rules?"

I made a few other such misspeaks and decided that silence was probably better than revealing my ignorance. My classes included French which I had studied in my high school with a Haitian teacher and therefore learned his pronunciation and idioms. I learned quickly that those limitations combined with my Alabama accent rendered my spoken French totally unacceptable in the classroom of my Sorbonne-educated Fisk professor! More silence. I had a similar setback in my freshman Humanities class with Robert Hayden. I was enthusiastic about the class but there were several students in it who graduated from the prestigious Latin School of Chicago. They often made references to readings they had done and how they related to our assigned reading. Even though I had always been an avid reader, my choices were not on par with those that they referenced. I was totally intimidated when a discussion hinged upon the word onomatopoeia. Not only could I not figure it out by any recognizable root words but had no idea how to spell it so a stop at the huge dictionary in the library was too time consuming!! (Yes, I just Googled it to spell it correctly here.)

Friday evening quiet hour in the chapel was soothing and very much appreciated as were Dean Faulkner's Sunday sermons. Most of the Basic College students participated in the Ford Theatre Guild. We were able to learn various aspects of play production and the opportunity to be part of a drama group had great appeal for me as theatre had been and continues to be my favorite entertainment genre.

We Dunn House girls shared talk of our "crushes" and mine was on a Basic College student, Quinn. With some strategizing a date to see a movie was arranged. (No ongoing dating followed but Quinn did escort me to the B.C. prom.)

We attended football and basketball games, went to the coop for snacks, listening to "Money Honey" on the jukebox and socializing. In our rooms we taught each other dance moves, studied, talked of possible careers and quickly the school year came to an end.

Summer Comes and Goes

My father had been asked to take an early retirement from his position as head of the Department of Secondary Education at Talladega. He was to be replaced by a professor with a doctorate. There was no consideration of the fact that his daughter had three more years of college yet to be paid for! Through educator friends he had made over the years, he secured a job at Tuskegee University and for my mother there was a position as resident advisor at the nursing dorm of the John Andrews Hospital.

A decision was made that their final retirement home would be in Raleigh, North Carolina. So tasks for the summer were to get household goods to Raleigh, begin to research where the new home would be built and return me to Nashville and themselves to Alabama.

After a long day's drive to Raleigh, we arrived at the hotel where we planned to stay. My dad went in and found it unacceptable. Options were limited; this was in days of segregation. I spoke up that I had a Fisk friend in Raleigh, Barbara, and that her father was the head of the State School for the Blind and Deaf. My dad lit up because he felt an immediate kinship with the head of a school. We found a way to make telephone contact with Barbara Crockett and her parents did not hesitate to give us directions to find their home on the campus. We asked for available space in one of the campus dorms but the Crocketts graciously made room for us in their home and a lasting friendship which included many bridge games was forged between the families.

The following November, Barbara and I traveled from Fisk to Raleigh to be presented in the Alpha Kappa Alpha Debutante Ball. My mother called upon her schoolteacher niece in Durham to find my escort for the big formal event. Several other activities were scheduled and Barbara and I showed our skill at dancing the Funky Chicken at informal parties.

Remaining Fisk Years

In my second year I was living in Jubilee Hall in a room on the front of that historic building overlooking the Oval and my roommate was "Jacqui Mac." We bonded, sang "Candy Kisses Wrapped in Paper" with the correct twang, sock-feet up against the wall and had a great time. When serenades and/or panty raids were performed by the fraternity guys on the Oval we had front-row "seats"!

I had made no advances in adequate study habits unfortunately. I have recently found a letter that Dean St. John, Head of the Basic College, sent to my parents stating that I had tested high but did not reflect this in my academic performance. I wish that letter had been directed to me as I did not realize what an academic disgrace my record was but just went sailing along learning what and where my interests lay but without exerting myself or focusing on improving my performance.

The following year found me with roommate Hildred Roach living in Bennett Hall. It was good to be close to Chase Hall, the science building where I had many classes as I had decided on a major in zoology. Fortunately, I did have a decent enough grade point average to qualify for Alpha Kappa Alpha Sorority pledging and on October 5, 1955, both Hildred and I got the awaited letter to appear in Jubilee Hall dressed in white. This began my induction into Pi Chapter. I had not calculated the number of my cousins, five, or that my dear Aunt Jessie were all Sorors of AKA. Pledging brought experiences such as going off campus with our brother Alpha pledgees to drink Champale at local eateries, running errands for big sisters and memorizing large amounts of the history of the sorority. Crossing the "burning sands" to become a Soror of AKA was one of the best ventures I've ever made. I find that often when I meet new people and gravitate toward them it turns out they are my AKA Sorors.

Romance Looms

My roommate, Hildred, had achieved fame in her home state of North Carolina and beyond for her talent as a pianist and we found ourselves being joined at meals by Tom Rozzell, a freshman, also a Carolinian, who expressed his interest in getting to meet the acclaimed musician. When he also turned up in my lab time at the science building it was revealed that his interest was not in the musician but the science student.

I was never a good student in mathematics, excluding geometry, but it went downhill when Tom Rozzell showed up enrolled in the same physics class taught by Dr. Gertrude Remfer. The distraction did me no good grade wise but by that time I had encountered enough organic chemistry to realize that med school would not be in my future.

Tom and I were to attend my senior prom held at Meharry's cafeteria. We were double dating with his roommate Ken Lockett and girlfriend June Radford. The guys, wanting to make the evening special, sent a bottle of Port to Brown's Hotel where we were to have a pre-prom dinner. Dinner with a quarter of a bottle of Port for each inexperienced drinker put us all in sleep mode. We did get to the dance but were so drowsy that we soon left and I was back in my dorm room before 11 P.M.

Career Choices and Graduation

In the summer after my second and third Fisk years I put my Camp Atwater experience to use by taking a job as a camp counselor at Camp Jawonio in New York State. It was sponsored by the United Cerebral Palsy Association. I enjoyed working with the campers, doing the daily care of kids my age and younger with physical disabilities, mostly cerebral palsy. Counselors also took turns assisting speech, occupational and physical therapists who worked with the campers. Since I was from so far away several of the other counselors invited me to their Long Island or Brooklyn homes when we had our days off. I remember how I enjoyed seeing the Cloisters on one such visit. It was amazing to me that these teens navigated NYC on their own.

When I went home to Tuskegee for Christmas holidays in my Fisk senior year I had decided on Occupational Therapy as a career. My dad took me to meet the occupational therapist at the veterans' hospital and they were working on attaching broom straws to handles. There were other such job skills being facilitated but since I wanted to work in pediatrics and had envisioned more craft-type activities that ended my interest in OT. My focus then turned to Physical Therapy as a career.

One more almost disastrous Fisk adventure was in a required-for-graduation philosophy course which I found absorbing and thought provoking. I was my consistently silent self during the class sessions but worked really hard on the required final paper. It was an analysis of Plato's "Allegory of the Cave." It was so well done that Dr. Buchanan was sure someone had ghost-written it! I was called to his office for stern talk about cheating, honor, etc., but I was given a chance to show that I'd read the material and discuss my insights regarding points I had made in my paper. Whew!!! We had a great exchange of ideas about the meaning of the allegory and other writers' ideas about life. My grade for the paper and the course was an A+!

Of course, commencement was attended by my parents and it was the fortieth anniversary of my mother's graduation. She was surprised and pleased that one of her classmates also had a daughter in the graduating class of 1957. Great celebration.

U. Penn and Philly

I was lucky to get scholarship funding from the March of Dimes to help with costs for the Physical Therapy Certification program. Penn did not have on-campus housing for students in the School of Auxiliary Medical Services so referred me to Mrs. Wilma Blake who provided room and board for Negro students in the program. I was the only student who lived in her home at the time. "Jake," the mother of Mrs. Blake, made my meals and I was quite comfortable in my Green St. lodgings. My hosts were migrants from GA and insisted that I was being "funny" when I said I had never eaten scrapple growing up in Alabama!

My classes at Penn included undergraduates. Anatomy classes were held at the medical school where we used cadavers already dissected since undergrads could not do dissection by Pennsylvania law. Students in the Occupational Therapy as well as the PT program were in these classes. This is where I met Carrie Fitten, a transplant from Georgia as well as an AKA Soror. I was happily surprised when, after I attended church at Westminster Methodist, she came up to welcome me and invite me to her house for coffee. Well, there was her sister's fantastic poundcake to go with the coffee and we made it a regular after church event, usually spending a few hours or so studying together.

My mother connected me with some Bullock relatives that lived in Philly and they were also warm and hospitable. I especially liked one cousin, Martha Bernadino, a nurse, because she had my grandmother's name and was not much older than I.

When money ran tight, I went to the Penn office for student employment and found a job with flexible hours at the apartment of a grad student whose wife was expecting their second child and was on semi-bedrest. This was in late spring of 1958 and Tom got a summer job at Union Carbide Company there in Philly. Much of our time together was spent with him helping me mop floors and with the other housekeeping/babysitting chores I had taken on.

Only one of my instructors in the PT program was enthusiastic about pediatrics as a specialty in therapy practice, Rheta Adams. I think I was the only student that was determined to head in that direction. When observational clinical practice began, I was assigned to St. Christopher's Hospital for Children and loved it. Next was my general hospital assignment at the University Hospital where one of my patients was in an iron lung (polio treatment). She did not survive. I was in high hopes of getting to do my internship at the Children's Seashore House in Atlantic City, NJ. My assignment was instead at Valley Forge Army Hospital. The only thing good about that was that my rank as a PT meant I was to eat in Officers Mess. I later learned that the Atlantic City facility did not want Negro students because they had "no housing" for them!!!!

Out into the World

I completed my studies and was a Certified Physical Therapist looking for a job. My parents had built their home, "Gay Acres," on a wooded plot in Garner, NC, just out of Raleigh. We knew that there would be no jobs for a Black PT in the local hospitals. Family friends thought it might be a good idea for me to push for a job in a VA hospital so I could stay in NC but VA work was not appealing to me nor was a possible legal battle. In response to inquiries, I received a job offer from St. John's Hospital in Springfield, IL.

I had visited with my Aunt Jessie when she lived in Chicago, had not been in other parts of IL, but the state did use the slogan "Land of Lincoln." The hospital housed the Downstate Children's Contagious Ward and that sounded right up my alley so off I went.

Since I was engaged to marry Tommy Rozzell, I did not feel the need to set up an apartment for the expected short time I would be in Springfield so I moved into the Rita Club where student nurse anesthetists, some nurses and other female hospital workers lived. We were under the eye of the order of nuns who ran the residence and I was under the eye of the huge statue of Christ at the end of the hall where my room was. His face was seen through the transom over my room door.

The physical therapy department had one male PT, one male exercise therapist, and was headed by Sister Mary Martin, who often invited me to the convent for weekends. Of this crew none were interested in battling me to work with the pediatric patients in the contagious ward. I had the opportunity to work with a Black teen who was recovering from echo cocksackie virus, similar to polio (now eradicated). She and I were used by the March of Dimes to further their fundraising so Dorothy and I "made the papers!!"

I first observed the clinical use of hypnosis in the PT department. A construction worker had fallen from a ladder suffering no detectable injuries but no longer able to walk or stand. It was decided that he had psychological paralysis and it was arranged for him to undergo a series of hypnotic sessions. Several of us were allowed to observe this approach and, yes, he did regain the ability to ambulate.

New Friends

I liked exploring the historic/Lincoln sites of Springfield but its underbelly was not pretty. I did not accept the invites to the convent for weekends, but found Grace Methodist Church and there made a BFF in LaVon Woodson Wilson. A native of Springfield, she and her husband, LaMar, had graduated from Lincoln University, in MO, and were raising son LaMar Jr. I hung out at their home, got to know her mom and later became Godmother to their younger son, Mark. I joined the Wilsons on a road trip to St. Louis where we went to a Chinese restaurant, a first for me. We also went to Hannibal, MO, for the Mark Twain trail.

The underbelly referred to was that hiring of LaVon as a public schoolteacher was for a long time denied because of race. Another thing I came to realize was that I could eat in any of the local places with a group of the other Rita Club residents, who all happened to be White, but when Tom came to visit and we went to Caputo's, one of my favorites when with the group, they were suddenly "reservation only" even though 90% empty and no tables marked "Reserved"!

Marriage and So On

Tommy and I had selected December of 1959 for our wedding since many of our friends were in grad school and would be available to attend over the Christmas break. This was his situation as well since he was in Kettering School at the University of Cincinnati working toward his Master's degree. Barbara Crockett and Jane Fort, of Fisk's Dunn House, and Carrie Fitten, my Philly friend, all AKA Sorors, were my attendants. We planned to see ex-roommate Hildred on the honeymoon in NYC where we would catch parts of the Omega Convention where she would be performing. My Soror cousin, Kathryn Bullock, was wedding soloist and Angela Gay Fox, child of my parents' friends, was flower girl.

Tom was attended by his brother, Marion Anthony; Fisk roommate, E. Wellington Butts; high school-student-government friend Ronald Schooler; and Fisk friend James Oxley.

Aunt Jessie produced a lovely rehearsal meal for the group and other out-of-town visitors. Another first for me was that my pals "did" my nails that evening. No surprise, the dresses were shades of pink and green.

I was possibly giddy but I think the church ceremony went off without a hitch, we returned home to Gay Acres for a reception of punch and light fare then a grand sendoff at the Raleigh train station and on to NYC. We saw "Flower Drum Song" on Broadway, checked out other NYC sights and went to the Omega convention dance.

Cincinnati and New Lives

The first job at hand was for me to find a job to add funds to the student stipend that Tom was receiving. This was an unexpected challenge for I learned that the administrator of Christ Hospital said the only "colored person" he would hire would be kitchen help. This was told to me by the administrator of the hospital that did hire me, Bethesda Hospital. In my interview with the head of the PT Dept., Ann Ferris, the main question was if I would have a problem with her being "the boss" since I had more work experience than she did. No. We soon became BFF and work there was a good experience despite not being pediatric centered.

Tom obtained his Master's and began work at Taft Sanitary Engineering Center just outside the city. He was an officer in the U.S. Public Health Service but was not in uniform. Sometimes I told people I met where he worked and they thought because of the name "Sanitary" that he was a garbageman.

When I became pregnant, medical care was available from the medical service at Wright Patterson Air Force Base in Dayton. Of course, a local MD was needed and I was lucky to find just the right person with an office near our new apartment. Lucy Oxley, MD, was also a relative of Leo and James Oxley that we knew from Fisk and Meharry. She said that the most modern facility where she had practice privilege was the Salvation Army's Catherine Booth Hospital and asked if I objected to having my baby delivered there. The reason for the question was that it was also a home for unwed mothers. Not a problem, except there was no waiting room for fathers and after the Christmas evening birth of Liane in 1960, the staff wanted to let Tom know and since he didn't answer the home phone they were trying to rouse me to find out where he could be located to report her birth.

I had a problem with that hospital staff when our second child, Eric, was born in 1963. Liane had been attending a preschool as I had taken a part-time PT job and she had given me the mumps. When labor started, I went to the hospital with a slight fever and the nursing staff said horrible things about a pregnant woman who "let" herself catch the mumps. We were "contaminated." Eric's bassinette was in my room and whoever came in to do the routine care grumbled mightily about having to don the isolation gear, etc. I was glad to leave to go home with my healthy baby son.

I finally got my desired pediatric job at the Cerebral Palsy Center on Victory Parkway. There were monthly clinics held by Dr. Aaron Perlman who was known for his work with children with cerebral palsy so I learned much there.

My mother, who had come to be with us each time we brought a new baby home, visited often as she and her friend Mrs. Stanley traveled to congregational churchwomen's meetings. Mrs. Stanley's son, Thomas, worked at Taft Center and he and his wife Joan, a Fiskite, had become our friends. The two grandmothers were known for planning their church-lady trips to always go by way of Cincinnati.

Return to School

We had purchased a home for the second time, made friends and settled comfortably but the lure of a terminal degree led us to leave Cincinnati for Tom to enroll in the Graduate School of Public Health at University of Pittsburgh. Much planning by some Pitt staff and friends had gone on before the invitation for our move. Prepped for our arrival was our living space, the ground floor of a duplex in the Squirrel Hill neighborhood, a mostly Jewish area near the university, shops, good schools, etc. I was set up with an evening job at the university library pending my finding work in the Physical Therapy field.

Close to our house was the Home for Crippled Children and I soon became a staff physical therapist there and held that post for four years. Virginia Whitfield, the Chief PT, had trained in London with the Bobaths whose methodology was making waves as the best approach to successfully produce better motor skills in children with cerebral palsy.

Not only did I have a great job but my Fisk roomie Jacqui was living in Pittsburgh with husband Alan and son Tony. What fun it was to get together for family picnics, dinners and other gatherings. At the end of the day of the funeral service for MLK, Jacqui delivered her daughter, Jennifer, and I became her Godmother!

Jacqui and I put our interests and talents in crafts together with others who had the entrepreneurial spirit and established the "Nine Women Show and Sale" event.

My parents did not visit us in Pittsburgh as my mother had been diagnosed with aplastic anemia and was being treated at Duke Hospital. I went to Raleigh as often as I could and realized that Dad's congestive heart problem was also an issue. Tom's studies limited his freedom to get to North Carolina to visit either set of our parents. Health situations continued to get worse, Momma, after having a stroke, was admitted to Triangle Nursing Center and caregivers were hired to help Dad with his food and household activities. Finally, in December of 1967 after failure of a transfusion for the anemia, my mother was admitted to Duke Hospital where she passed away. I will always be grateful that Aunt Jessie was there with us during that time.

We packed up Dad's things, closed the house and returned to Pittsburgh, where Dad had a final heart attack, passing away 29 days after my mother. He was ready; he said he was "ready."

Settling

Tom was awarded his D.Sc. from Pitt and stayed on as a faculty member of the Graduate School of Public Health. We purchased a house in our same neighborhood. I could ride my bike to work at the Home for Crippled Children, Liane and Eric were in a good school. We bought a small boat docked on the Ohio River, and continued to go on family camping trips.

We decided that we would like to give a home to an adopted child. A social worker visited and Li and Eric expressed their choices of a sibling. Girl or boy? Before a decision was made it turned out that I was pregnant!

One hitch was that I developed excruciating oral pain. Eating and speaking were nearly impossible because of intense pain which was finally diagnosed as trigeminal neuralgia. The most used medication was, I found when I researched, possibly toxic to a fetus. Someone that heard of my dilemma knew of a clinical psychologist at Duquesne University who used hypnosis and taught self-hypnosis for pain control. Remembering my observation years ago in Springfield I contacted this psychologist, learned the technique and was greatly pleased to find relief. When I spoke to my obstetrician he approved and said he used hypnosis for delivering babies and we could do that. We did! A surprise was that there were extra people in the delivery room to observe because it was not that common an event!!!

So our last child, Jon "Kofi," was born. Aunt Jessie came to welcome him as my mother had done for the other children.

An Offer We Couldn't Refuse

We were enjoying our life in Pittsburgh but an offer came for Tom to work at the Office of Naval Research in Arlington, Virginia. We had talked about various places we'd like to live but Virginia was not on the list. The magic factor was that a two-year overseas assignment was part of the deal. We'd heard of the planned community Reston, VA, which sounded appealing so we began to plan the move. Reston was much too far from the Arlington office so was ruled out. We were so used to being close to work and city amenities. We made several weekend trips to Virginia to find a suitable place. We were dealing with prejudices as we were told we "would not be comfortable" in this or that neighborhood. Late on a Sunday afternoon as we headed, discouraged, for the highway we passed an expanding development of contemporary homes and both said, "Let's just go look." The person in the model home/sales office rose, quickly offered a handshake and said, "Are you looking for a home?" Ken Murphy took us to see the available lots, driving us around the Truro neighborhood, pointing out his own home and before heading back to Pittsburgh we had selected our Virginia home.

After organizing our new home, getting Liane, sixth grade, and Eric, third grade, settled into school, I became active as a volunteer driver for people who had medical appointments and no transportation. It was a great way to learn my way around the area and my toddler was content to be in his car seat during these excursions. At times the appointments were as far as the Georgetown Dental clinic in D.C.

Soon, I wanted to work as a PT again so found a preschool for Jon and began work for the Fairfax County Health Department providing services at two schools which served physically handicapped students.

I became active in the local unit of the League of Women Voters again as I had been in Pittsburgh. My craft skills were used in many PTA projects. Tom and I found our interest in theater could be more easily afforded by volunteering as ushers at Folger Shakespeare Theater and Arena Stage.

During his time at the Office of Naval Research, Tom attended what were known at the "Winter Brain Conferences." These were held yearly at various ski resorts and he thoroughly enjoyed them. When he proposed that we ski as a family group, I was not convinced but the advantage of a sport that each could do at various levels won me over. Our first try was with a Department of Defense group, a bus trip to Big Vanilla in NY State. It went well and next time we ventured to Breckenridge, CO, and it was even better. My final trip to ski was with the Potomac Valley Ski group combining a sightseeing trip to Barcelona, Spain, with skiing in the Pyrenees in the tiny country of Andorra.

Late Blooming

In 1974 an opportunity came to work at the Child Development Center of Northern Virginia.

The consultant that held monthly clinics there was Burton Chance, M.D., one of the East Coast's most renown specialists in pediatric physical medicine. There were three preschool classrooms and an infant program. Truly my dream job! In 1978 I was promoted to chief therapist when my dear friend Aurelia Mayer left the position due to cancer.

I attended many continuing education courses and was able to get my full certification in the Bobath technique, known as Neurodevelopment Treatment (NDT), at the University of Maryland, Baltimore. This was done in a summer of eight weeks of daily commuting. Two other therapists and I took turns driving the carpool! The director of the center assisted by arranging for her nursing school student daughter to be babysitter for my three children during this summer adventure.

I organized the Advanced Baby Course in NDT held at the center in 1983 and in that year, while continuing to hold my job, I enrolled at George Washington University in a course leading to the Master's Degree in Education and Human Development. In that program I was a straight-A student with many commendations from my instructors on the excellent quality of my work, on my insights and diligence and in sharing with others my knowledge and expertise. With all this activity I was also involved in organizing and then becoming a charter member of the Lambda Kappa Omega Chapter of Alpha Kappa Alpha along with a lovely energetic group of Northern Virginia Sorors.

Overseas Adventure

Just as my return to education was being completed the offered travel was scheduled and we were moving to England where Tommy was to work in the Office of Naval Research, Marylebone Station, London.

The family at this point included Aunt Jessie who had continued to live with us following the death of husband, Robert Thornton. Younger son "Kofi," Jon, entered the American School, London (ASL), where he attended the eighth and ninth grades. Having finished college, Liane was writing for and editing a magazine in D.C. and Eric was in aeronautical studies at Kent State University, Ohio.

I felt the need to engage with other parents of ASL students to determine how a suburban American teen should be guided in London! This is how I met Betty Flood, an ASL mom who had a raffle quilt underway and offered to teach me to quilt in exchange for my help with her project. I helped, she taught and I was "hooked" on quilting!

In trying to see how "physiotherapy" was practiced in the National Health System of the U.K. I took a job at Paddington Green Children's Hospital. I had intended to be a tourist for the two years abroad but my post as the "foreign physio" included 15 days' leave from the point of hiring. I had to take emergency calls on some weekends but could be anywhere in the 400 square miles of greater London during on call times, carrying my walkie-talkie. Additional leave time was given for on-call days and the American School believed in the educational value of travel so they encouraged students to do family trips. We took full advantage of these perks and our first Thanksgiving weekend in the UK found us in France and Germany!

I had met British citizen Debbie Lamb as a coworker at the Child Development Center. She had started my instruction in English versus

American and it was fun to continue to develop my vocabulary. When working with a child at Paddington Green you asked them to roll the "lorry" not to push the "truck!" A "boot sale" had nothing to do with footwear! We had Sunday lunch at Debbie's home and learned that a walk in Kew Gardens was not deterred by a bit of rain.

Return to Virginia

It was hard to leave my coworkers at Paddington Green who knew that the American Physio loved Bakewell Tart and let me know whenever it was "on offer" at the hospital cafeteria. One of my parting gifts was a cookbook with the recipe for the Bakewell Tart.

After seeing much of western Europe from our base in London we returned to our Fairfax, Virginia, home. Tommy worked for a few more years at the Office of Naval Research, I accepted an offer to work with special needs students in the Alexandria City Public Schools and Kofi entered Woodson High School.

Aunt Jessie decided that she wanted the companionship of other seniors and moved to an apartment in a continuing care facility.

I joined a local quilters group and we expanded our skills in cutting up fabric and sewing it together again. Arena Stage ushering was resumed and I joined in activities of the local Fisk Alumni group. After I assisted with recruitment of future Fiskites at local college fairs, my mentor in this activity retired, and handed recruitment materials over to me.

Liane continued working and living in D.C. Eric finished his studies at Kent State and took his first airline job, based in Springfield, Illinois!! Soon Eric married, moved to Phoenix, Arizona, and presented us with grandkids Alexis and Nick.

Liane found her life partner in Linda Kaufman and their marriage ceremony included Ryan, who was already son to Linda. They later added Jamal to their family. The delightful little Josiah, son of Ryan, joined the family as did Dwayne, a smart and thoughtful teen nephew adopted by Jamal.

Travel Configurations

Tom, having taken a position at the National Academy of Sciences, had many work-related travel opportunities. We shared the idea that having seen many European countries, we should see the states in the U.S. that we had not yet visited so we made use of the free flights available due to being "dependents" of pilot son Eric. Nebraska and North Dakota were the states that completed our tour of the 50! This was one of our last trips together as the marriage flame was sputtering out and Tom soon moved from the family home.

I tested my wings for solo travel with a trip to Machu Pichu! I spent two weeks one February on St. Kitts volunteering with a team documenting information useful to genealogists and family historians from burials in one of the island cemeteries.

Influenced by hearing of Miss Lillian Carter's Peace Core experience, I found a way to serve, learn and travel in short stints through an organization, Global Volunteers (GV). I spent two weeks in Mitera, Tanzania, working in a boarding middle school with no running water and dedicated students for my first GV trip. A few days seeing Zanzibar preceded that. Weeks after 9/11 I joined a medical team of Global Volunteers to spend two weeks in Xi'an, China, sharing information with our counterparts at the Shaanxi Provincial Hospital and teaching conversational English. I tacked a five-day sightseeing stint in Beijing on to that trip, since I did not expect to return to China. Most of our group also visited the Terra Cotta Warriors. With great excitement I signed up for a GV trip of two weeks in Salvador, Bahia, Brazil and added sightseeing in Rio to that one.

When granddaughter Alexis had reached the age of ten, wanting to interact with her more I signed us up for a Road Scholar Intergenerational trip. We saw Lake Tahoe, stayed in a Sierra Club lodge, learned about the Donner Party and the building of the transcontinental railroad. Alexis was a good travel companion so another summer we took a trip that included Best Friends Animal Sanctuary in Utah, Zion and Bryce Canyon Parks. Our next trip was further afield as the pair of us went to Ecuador on a Global Volunteers program working in a preschool near Quito.

Grandson Nick and I enjoyed an Intergenerational trip where we rode the NYC subways, saw Aladdin on Broadway, Wall St., etc. His choice instead of joining the proposed group walk across the Brooklyn Bridge was to visit the grand opening of a guitar store!

Nick, Alexis and I joined up for a week on a Global team in Cuba and our most recent trip was organized by Eric who invited me to join him and Alexis taking Nick to Valencia, Spain, for the first year of Nick's college enrollment (Berklee College of Music).

Life Changes

In 1998, after a stroke and declining health my dear Aunt Jessie passed away. Tom, who had looked forward to travel in retirement, also was sidelined by health issues and died shortly after his 81st birthday.

Soon after returning to Fairfax, I had begun to spend a day that stretched from sign-in at 5 A.M. to heading home around 9 P.M. as an elections officer. I like this act of civic participation which occurs usually twice per year. I have served in this role for more than thirty times. I did not know until I recently started family history research that my great-grandfather, Benjamin Johnson, was an elections officer (and justice of the peace) in the 1860s in North Carolina!

After 27 years of work in the city schools I felt like Alexandria was a "hometown" for me and I volunteered in its Black History Museum before and after retirement. Also, I found being a weekly volunteer at nearby Fairfax Inova Hospital provided exercise and satisfaction. It is a large building complex in which to do patient discharges and other errands.

I am a member of four book groups and have a continuing, long list of books to read. Sometimes digging through census records for genealogical research and working my way through my reading lists limits my time to sleep!! Many activities have been curtailed due to the current pandemic (2020-2021). Some, such as my valued weekly yoga class and most of the book groups, have transitioned to Zoom.

Meeting with the metro area Fisk Alumni group on Zoom saves a lot of commuting time but I am proud to say that pre-pandemic, in 2018, at the Talented Tenth Gala I was one of the awardees receiving the Hassell H. McClellan Award Recognizing Dedication to Fisk. My Fisk Family remains very important to me.

As I await the next adventures that come, I can only say it has been an interesting journey and I am thankful for all the experiences that have made me the woman I am today. To those I've known I say I'm so glad we had these times together.

Lula Bullock Gay and Wolsey Gay with five-month-old Maryann

Then and Now

with granddaughter

with grandchildren

At Annapolis Sailing School

On the slopes of Snowmass

With friends and students in Mtera Tanzania

grandson

Hildred Roach

I am Hildred Roach, a native of Charlotte, North Carolina. As the daughter of a farmer's widow, my story is different from those of my Fisk sisters. Yet an overview of my life will reveal that I became a pianist, retired educator, founder of Group Three (an ensemble devoted to the performance of music by Pan African composers), author of *Black American Music:* Past *and Present* and *Profiles of Strong Proud People* (my roots, unpublished). As a grateful recipient of Ford Foundation's Early Entrant Scholarship program to Fisk University, supplemented by funds from the sixth district Omega Psi Phi Fraternity, I became the first in my immediate family to attend college in 1953. When I was sixteen, that was the year I would have begun my senior year on scholarship at Lincoln Academy High School. Although I realized the significance of the grants, I nevertheless experienced fear of the unknown and an uncertainty about the unusual plan to start something new without first having finished the old. I sprang from very humble beginnings and could not fathom before that time how I would ever attend college. It goes without saying that an offer to study at Fisk as a basic college student for four straight years was a rare opportunity that just could not be refused.

Key accomplishments were: a Bachelor of Music from Fisk University, in 1957, cum laude, complete with Phi Beta Kappa and Alpha Kappa Alpha Sorority memberships and a Sarah Mckim Maloney Award; a Master of Music degree from Yale in 1962, complete with a scholarship and loan (which I paid back before graduating); a Yale Lockwood scholarship Award (monetary and opportunity to perform a concerto under the baton of Gustav Meier); 1960 scholarships from the John Hay Whitney Foundation and the State of Alabama. Further studies included a year at the Juilliard School of Music, sponsored by Fisk Trustee Margaret Rieser in 1958; research at the University of Ghana in Legon, sponsored by the American Forum in summer, 1969 (where I met Margaret Burroughs, artist from Chicago, with other leaders Rev. Lawrence Jones and Dr. Eric Lincoln in command, and Dr. Kwabena Nketia as a lecturer); summer research on Pan-African Music in the Caribbean, sponsored by a University of D.C. CARUP Grant in 1985; study at Oakland in Michigan at the Isaac Stern-Leonard Rose-Eugene Istomin Trio workshops; and postgraduate studies with master teachers William Masselos (who had performed at Fisk years ago) and Bela Nagy from Catholic University, and Fernando Laires from the University of Maryland (which institution awarded grants to its piano festivals).

During my work as either student or teacher, I performed piano solo concerts at Lincoln Academy High School, Livingstone College, Fisk University, Tuskegee Institute, Yale University, Fayetteville State College, Virginia State College, Howard University and the University of D.C., etc.; several ensemble concerts with graduate students at Yale, with faculty and students at all of the Universities where I taught, Trio concerts at public schools in Gaston County, N.C., with Group Three (Nelda Ormond, soprano; Norma Hunton, violin); several concerts with Pro Viva Trio (Antoinette Handy, founder-flutist, and Ron Lipscomb, cellist); duo piano recitals with Dr. Marva Cooper (in N.C. and the Washington Metro area) and with Dr. Percy Gregory and Harvey Van Buren Jr. in D.C. and with the latter, several Omega Conclaves in various U.S. cities. In Pan-African music, I gave both solo and ensemble lecture-demonstrations in D.C., at Music Educators Conventions during the 1970s-2000s, and also with Dr. Oscar Henry, tenor (one of which was held in D.C. at the Congressional Wives Mansion). Among other honors received were a Yale Merit Award in 1982, and listings in *Outstanding Educators of America*, *Who's Who in Maryland*, and Dr. Eileen Southern's *Biographical Dictionary*.

How did such blessings transpire? Who else was responsible for countless decisions and continuous assistance that made it possible to transform a life of such an unsure little introvert from her smallest beginnings imaginable to such an exciting career? Who else in my unique background besides God lifted me up and brought me to the point where I could eventually not only stand on my own two feet these many years later, but also contribute to the welfare of others? Here is my unusual American story.

MY FOREBEARS count a lot in describing me as much as the culture in which I was raised. The earliest of my ancestors found on my maternal side were my great-grandparents, Robert Caldwell Sr. (ca. 1830-1900) and his wife, Nancy Sample (ca. 1830-1905). Legend and fact place Robert as a slave on John Davidson's Mecklenburg County Plantation, situated about twenty miles northwest of Charlotte, North Carolina— "up in the Neck," they called it—where ferries carried slaves "to and fro" on the Catawba River. Nancy, once a slave of W. A. Sample, and owners of the Latta Plantation were listed alongside Robert in the Hopewell Presbyterian Church Directory where slaves worshipped in the balcony. Described by my mother as "a White-looking woman," she was either an indentured servant or a mulatto. It is plausible to assume that she was the latter since marriage between different races was unlawful in the U.S.

John Davidson himself was born in Lancaster County, Pennsylvania, in 1735, to parents who "had emigrated from Scotland in 1729." Surprisingly, according to a White student enrolled at Davidson College who cowrote a 2017 sociology class research paper at Johnson C. Smith University with my great niece, Ebony Hill et al, Davidson was her sixth great-grandfather who moved from Pennsylvania with his mother to Mecklenburg County and built a small log cabin on the banks of the Catawba River. In time, his daring ventures "morphed" into a large plantation with an ornate house on Neck Road, which he named "Rural Hill." He became a justice of the peace, dealt in farming, politics, the militia and, as was the common practice in the antebellum south, participated in the ever-growing, lucrative slave trade—which is how my great-grandpa Robert Sr. and his brothers somehow landed on the Davidson property.

Indeed, Davidson was also a member of the group which founded Davidson College, and a member of Hopewell Presbyterian Church on Huntersville Road (whose staff allowed me to take pictures of the balcony where my ancestors worshipped). He also fathered ten children. When his daughter, Sarah, married David Alexander Caldwell, Robert Sr. was evidently gifted to that family, thus exchanging the Davidson surname for that of Caldwell, while his brothers Perry and William remained on the Davidson property. Fortunately, the brothers were kept in close enough contact to remember their kin, and likewise settled in close proximity after the Civil War.

My maternal grandparents were Robert Caldwell Jr. (ca. 1856-1930) and Mary ("Molly") Ramseur (ca. 1863-1934), whose exact origins were equally difficult to trace as were those of their parents. It was said that she came from nearby Lincolnton and had met Robert Jr. at a dance. (It is amusing for me to contemplate that as contemporaries of Scott Joplin (1854-1917) they might have danced to the music of the famous "Ragtime King" whom I was researching in my Pan African studies). Their offspring told me that she was two or three years old "at surrender" and that Robert was about six. However, both may have been older, as later U.S. Census records are hard to collate. In any case, Robert Jr. was listed in his father's household on the 1880 Census as a twenty-four-year-old who could not read or write. (Family members whom I interviewed said that he and she had attended precursor institutions of Johnson C. Smith and Barber Scotia respectively. Needless to say, educational levels of older institutions were limited—as they were for the Fisk barracks of yesteryear—and records of those studies were either nonexistent or "buried in a box" by the time I inquired in the 1990s.) Nevertheless, both were represented as respected persons with good wits and inventiveness. The historical records of Nazareth Primitive Baptist Church hold that they were among the founders "when the Church was organized a few years after the Civil War in 1877, when a group of dedicated Christians met at the home of Brother Robert and Sister (Molly) Caldwell on Statesville Road...."

Their home on Statesville Road was a log cabin—a structure which must have been similar to the one used by John Davidson upon his arrival at the Catawba River. My mother recalled other interesting "tidbits" such as her father's role as a church official and trainer of the choir, who used "sol-fa" syllables and perhaps long and short meters, Isaac Watts and other methods in the teaching of hymn tunes. When choir practice was held, Mama sang alto in the choir and surely must have gleaned basic aural fundamentals of ear training and reading, for as a child, I was always impressed by her ability to blend such sure harmonies into pieces like "Amazing Grace" and her talent to improvise in the old customs of "lining out the notes."

Robert Jr., whose brothers helped build roads in Mecklenburg County using their horse teams, owned a horse named "Gray Charlie" which he entered into Charlotte Fair Races. Mama did not say whether he profited from the races, but luck certainly seemed to favor him. For example, after showing me where their old log cabin and flour mill once stood, she recalled that Grandpa Robert sold the cabin to a Caucasian and moved his family to property bought from Davidson College officials by the early 1900s. Situated on both sides of Rozzell's Ferry Road (Route 16) about ten miles northwest of Charlotte and in direct line to the Rozzell Ferry, it was in this place that Grandpa discovered a gold mine in the woods, carted the nuggets off to the Charlotte Mint—which the All-State Vacation Guide cited as "the nation's top gold mining center before the Gold Rush of California"—and where today, artworks by my niece Nellie Ashford ironically hang mirroring the past both there and on the walls of the airport terminal. The Mint was also near the First National Bank containing Grandpa's money. (Subsequently, the bank went bankrupt but began repaying the money either before or after Grandpa's death.) By the time I heard the story from Mama in the 1990s long after I graduated from Fisk "poorer than a church mouse," none of that money had ever crossed my path nor hers, for however much was repaid, Grandpa's older children had apparently claimed it all without sharing any such "stash" with us.

My parents were Howard Roach (ca. 1888-1938) and Pearl Caldwell Roach (1893-1993). Born during Reconstruction, Howard was the son of Prince Roach (ca. 1847-1916) and Violet Henderson (ca. 1860-1914) of Ebenezer Township in York County, S.C. According to Soundex Records, these paternal grandparents were farmers with no formal education, living on rented farmland. Papa left his father's farm and landed a job at a mill on the Yadkin River in Spencer, N.C., just north of Charlotte where Mama was born in Mecklenburg County. Whether they met at Zion Baptist (the "Mother Church"), Nazareth Primitive Baptist Church or the Camp Meeting in Tucker's Grove is not clear, but in any case, they were married and living in the Charlotte area by 1917 where Harold was first born, and then moved to Kittanning, Pennsylvania, where Clarence was born. Sometime later, they returned to farmland in Paw Creek, a "country suburb" of Charlotte, where I was born years later as the last of their brood. (At that point in the early 1900s, nobody had a clue that Harold would teach me to drive Mama's 1950 Chevrolet in preparation for work in Fayetteville, or that Clarence would drive me to the Davidson Plantation in the 1990s.)

"IT TAKES A VILLAGE" to raise a child, and in my case, the old adage rang entirely true. One year after my birth, Papa passed away in 1938 while in his late forties. "Smack dab" in the midst of the Depression and on the eve of World War II, the event immediately set off various reactions, and I was surrounded by supporters from family to many others. Key ones were: my brother Ervin, who "ran for the doctor" and teased me years later that if not for him, I would otherwise have been born on the wagon instead of at home; church members who quelled my vociferous cries at the funeral; ex-slave Sister Montgomery, who sewed a beautiful purple-and-yellow quilt for me; and others, both White and Black, who were sent like angels at seemingly every stage of my life.

There were Papa's elderly sisters, aunts Cora and Rosa (retired schoolteachers living in S.C. on Mountain View Road at the foot of Nanny's Mountain) who offered to attend the twins and me when they were five and I three. We enjoyed that they took us on short walks in the countryside, through their large garden, and to the freshwater spring down the hill near pretty white sand. But alas! The aunts had to bow out of the deal when they were frightened by our surprise disappearance from the front yard while they gathered vegetables in back. We had wandered from their driveway, meandered down the little red dirt road a mile or more, turned left onto Route 49 and headed north toward the Buster Boyd Bridge by the time they caught up to us in their T-Model Ford.

Then there was "Miz" Susie Graham, a kind neighbor married to Wilbert Graham, who resided on the middle part of Lawing School Road just over the high hill separating Lawing Road from the Rozzell Road area, who volunteered to keep me while Mama worked. With a keen mind, she continued the lessons that had begun at Mama's kitchen table: the little alphabet writing exercises, counting and number songs in call-and-response fashion (CALL: five, ten! RESPONSE: fifteen-twenty!) There was no preschool for us wee ones, but Susie and Mama did what they could. Miz Susie loved me as her own, and liked to "show me off." After I'd studied piano lessons for a year or so, she would interrupt my skipping to Mack Dunn's candy store, and beckon me to come play piano for her White employer, Mrs. Ed. Rozzell. (I felt the importance of being ushered into the front door of the living room where the piano stood, rather than to the back where Blacks would normally enter.) I'd reached early Bach and Clementi and was beginning to try WWII tunes and marches I'd heard on the radio. They seemed delighted to note my progress when they'd occasionally ask me to play. (In hindsight, I ponder if Miz Susie were a relative because she was so devoted to my upbringing, and who can tell how mixed up our lineages were as slave names were switched endlessly by countless sales?)

Miz Tommy Graham, whose husband, Ervin, was the brother of Wilbert Graham, was also an important neighbor who lived on our side of the area near Rozzell's Ferry Road. She intercepted the twins and me as we passed her home headed to the mailbox. Beaming with pride as an adult beginner, she showed us what she was learning on the piano. Watching in wide-eyed excitement, we were as happy as larks when she taught us a few black key tunes by rote. Thereafter, I evidently thought that it was my right to invite myself over to her home time and again to test and retest the sounds of her instrument—an intrusion which she tolerated for quite some time until she eventually offered to sell the unwieldy old upright "kerplunk-of-a-piano" to Mama for fifty dollars (whether to get me out of her house, or whether she thought I had musical promise, wasn't my concern at the time, for I was happy to get the object of my attention into easy possession, complete with its few disabled notes which disturbed no one in that moment in time). I was mesmerized and worked my ears into unimaginable realms of my own space, until Mama realized one day that I was "plunking out" real tunes. It was suggested that I study with Mrs. Carrie Robinson Quander, a high school music teacher who was absolutely on point in teaching chords and keys, alongside beginning literature and the hymn tunes I was eventually able to play in church. She and her sister Thelma, a nurse, were most kind and hospitable, occasionally inviting me to stay over in town for extra lessons, dinner, the public pool, movies and concerts (such as by Marian Anderson, Roland Hayes and an orchestra) and for showing countless things in the city which I never would have encountered in the country.

"MA PEARL," as her grandchildren called her, was my chief supporter, "cheerleader," the absolute love of my life and the essence of my being. Head of the household from 1938 onwards, she was a strict disciplinarian, and a churchgoing woman who raised her little ones with a "hickory stick" and a Bible. She taught us many lessons in manners, respect for elders, and honesty. My years of study took a bigger chunk of her time than was sane, but she never failed to send "care packages" and small spending sums, occasional clothes (especially the gowns for performing on stage), and she never failed to smile with evident pride upon my return home each semester. In the early 1980s, when it became necessary to move her from my Silver Spring home to the brick one inherited from Ervin—a handsome house I would have kept if not for the high taxes—her remaining children took turns lovingly caring for her. After having lived with me for twenty-three years, she was a centenarian when she passed away in 1993.

As the twelfth child in her father's family of thirteen, Ma Pearl could manage "facts and figures" in her head far better than we or her country peers. She could also cite Biblical "chapter and verse" better than most. Although the rural school system in Mecklenburg County in her time offered the Caldwell and other rural families only limited education as far as eighth grade, she mastered the subjects well enough to unofficially take over the classes of siblings and neighbors in the absence of their teachers during inclement weather. She loved "Finlandia" with its surprise hymn tune in the middle of the orchestral piece, Howard Thurmond's religious writings, the *Washington Post* ("Too much to read in a day," she'd say) and she often used appeggios on the piano to harmonize hymns by ear (which sent my nerves "a-scatter"). When I was eight, her keen hearing surprised me when she sang out corrections from the kitchen while I fumbled around missing notes on the piano in the adjacent room. (This method of locating notes she sang might have been how I developed "perfect pitch.") Practicing was my favorite thing to do at any time of the day, and was often a tactic used to escape garden and other chores; Mama encouraged regular practice by warning me that I was not to waste her "hard-earned money," so I complied.

With unusual "Mother Wit," sensitivity and sensibility, Mama could talk with ease to mostly anyone from "both sides of the aisle" (a characteristic Principal Annie Roberts described as her "personality plus") and could entice any baby in a crib to instantly break out in giggles and glee, and spritely little kicks. Quite the sage, she made difficult decisions on faith with the sure belief that "God would make a way out of no way" and would use quips like "What do YOU know? That's the way a motor sounds when it's ROAD Ready!" or "You can take a person out of the country but you can't take the country out of a person!" and directed to me, "A big-time college kid hanging kitchen curtains with the ruffles on the OUTSIDE?"

In 1941, three years after Papa's demise, she alone was responsible for the "talk" with her sons and daughters about police ("Don't argue with them! Just say, "Yes, sir!"). However, I somehow recall that these particular policemen in our small community did not carry the awful reputation of others elsewhere who were more mean-spirited, would haul you off to jail or yank you out of a car without adequate reason—or worse still, shoot or lynch you "in the blink of an eye." Instead, these men seemed to relish the show-off practice of just stopping people to impress them or were set on flexing their muscles, so to speak, to show "superiority" just to hear "Yes, SIR!" before issuing a speeding ticket.

Our community was mainly composed of blue-collar workers, and actually, the Caldwell and Davidson names were generally respected by the general population. So the relationship between races seemed civil enough as long as nobody from our side boasted about his worth or "talked back" with impudence. (Grandpa must have kept mum about his gold mine.) This "live and let live" attitude might have stemmed from the facts that the bitterness of the Civil War was not "an event" in Mecklenburg County, everybody knew everybody else, knew where families had been held those many years ago, and by whom. Therefore, I never heard of robed Klansmen burning crosses or riding horses in our area, although some were surely hiding in plain sight in business suits or "coveralls." Consequently, Freedmen in the community were left alone to pursue their own plans. Other reasons why our families might have been given a "pass" were: the shared religion of the Presbyterians and our forebears in the Hopewell Church balcony; the familiar names were not suspicious because the same parties still lived in close proximity to the plantations of "yesteryear," as the ex-slaves had settled within easy walking distance of those sites yet looming in the background. Also, the Black/White parties continued to do business with each other. For example, Mother's oldest brother, Ernest, walked with his cow "up Rozzell's Ferry Road" ever so often to mate with the White Caldwell's bull, just as their father, Robert Jr., had shown enough business acumen to negotiate the purchase of the Rozzell's Ferry Road real estate deal with the Davidson College family members, and in another instance, members of the Davidson College family had actually given property to our family for a church site. Furthermore, who can define the suppressed emotions and thoughts which the former "owners" might have felt about mixed procreation?

Long after the older members of Mama's family had left home to either marry or join the army, she chose to move the remainder of her children from Paw Creek to "Shuffletown" into a small house which was under construction when we moved in. This small house was made possible from funds sent by her military sons as well as from her own labor and served well as collateral. It was close to the farmland where Grandfather

Robert Jr. had settled on Rozzell's Ferry Road and the area consisted of mostly relatives and non-relatives of Grahams, Clarks, Caldwells, and Davidsons. Cousin John Harvey Davidson, whose father was Adolphus, rented a house on the other side of Rozzell's Ferry Road which he often rented to Whites.

Needless to say, nobody went hungry, for some men worked in the mills at Hoskins or Mt. Holly, while the ladies worked mostly as domestics, and all of these "farming families" kept small farms and/or large gardens which produced more than enough food for themselves and others to share. Mama taught us independence by growing our own food in gardens containing ample amounts of every imaginable vegetable or melon. Hidden out of sight in separate barns below our house were: pigs from which she made cured ham to store in the smokehouse and chickens which she used to cook into "mouth-watering" crunchiness, a friendly-looking "knock-kneed" cow who stared at us in seeming absentmindedness but who gave good milk to make churned butter for those yeast rolls, and an arrogant-acting mule who wouldn't allow anyone to place me on his back for a fun ride.

As a farmer's daughter, Mama knew how to teach her youngest son how to milk a cow and how to plow that haughty mule with "clicks, gee-haws, giddy-ups and whoa!" Her background included traditions melded together from African and American Indian cultures. Therefore, she could make lye soap for use in washtubs, and could point out various plants for medical remedies as well as edible ones such as wild greens, mushrooms, teas and spices. To us little kids settling into a new place, Mama was a courageous protector because of her multi-talents and ready answers to so many questions. She was also our "She-ro" who kept us safe because she was brave and knew how to do things like shooting Papa's shotgun into the sky whenever there were occasional little unidentified noises outside in the dark.

Ma Pearl also knew how to drive cars she purchased. For years she'd owned a T-Model Ford, and in later years, she got a kick out of boasting that she "was driving before you were born!" Buying cars during the 1940s and 1950s meant that we could avoid riding in the back of a bus, that she could drive me to the city for piano lessons and to choir rehearsals in town and back again for Wednesday night and Sunday morning services without much ado. This also meant a means of transportation with independence and pride in that she could drive on Saturdays to the McClure Lumber Company where we kids helped clean the offices, and to daily work at the Oakdale home of Herman and Margaret Anderson, owners of the juxtaposed Anderson Printing Press (who occasionally sent spending money to me while I was at Fisk and funded Mama's trip to Fisk upon my graduation. Also, one of Margaret's relatives named her daughter after Mama.).

Ma Pearl leaned on the "good word" and taught us children by rote the "Lord's Prayer" and the "Twenty-third Psalm." She bragged in the 1940s that when she and I once traveled by train to visit relatives in D.C., my recitations of Bible portions inspired passengers to give me enough change to pay the taxi fare from the station to Ruby's house. Her interest in Bible studies drew the attention of Hopewell Presbyterian Church, who sent her (with me in tow) to summer workshops lasting a week each summer for at least three years. Held at Winston-Salem Teachers College, she had the opportunity to do Bible studies with reputable female scholars, to earn certificates and to enjoy a mini-graduation, complete with cap and gown and broad smiles from us both.

Ultimately, Mama's other children became "blue-collar workers": Seven sisters worked as either cooks, caretakers, job counselors for the hardcore employed or garment factory worker; the brothers (all except the oldest who was a tailor at Ed Mellon's Department Store in Charlotte's Tryon-Trade "Square") became honorably discharged military men, then worked in construction as plasterers and brick masons. Luckily, two who helped brick the New York City Towers destroyed in the 9/11 disaster had already expired before the event, but unfortunately, cousin Bobby Moore, a security guard who escaped to his Long Island home, sat down at the table and passed away anyway. Although the deaths of her children who had helped build the Towers and a handsome brick rambler on Lawing School Road where she "lived out" her last days were difficult for Mama to suffer, she nevertheless lived through all of this trauma without experiencing a stroke. A survivor so aptly named Pearl, the mother of us all, really WAS a gem!

COUNTRY SCHOOLHOUSES counted as sites for my earliest education. The first was Lawing School Road Elementary, which Road was situated in perpendicular position to the Mt. Holly-Huntersville Road (splitting up into two directions at Route 16 heading north toward Hopewell Church and south toward Mt. Holly). Lawing Elementary was a two-room wooden building for grades one to six. Each room contained desks, blackboards, cloak room and a potbelly stove, but no other practical facilities either inside or out. Lawing School was about two miles northwest of Miz Susie's house, and was quizzically directly across the road from a graveyard where there was no church. From our neighborhood, we walked up the hill in a two-mile trek to school. (Little mountains seemingly always popped up in these childhood scenes.) Since there were no preschools available, I, at the age of five, tagged along behind the seven-year-old second-grade twins and thereupon met friendly Mrs. Cauley, who allowed me into her first-grade class if I promised to behave. A promise was kept, and this underaged first grader progressed to the second grade along with the others without much ado.

By 1948, I had completed the sixth grade, the last grade at Lawing, and was ready to move to the seventh. This time, we traveled on a ten-mile school bus trip to Woodland Elementary in Paw Creek as the County was closing Lawing Elementary and merging students from our area with those at Woodland in Paw Creek. The ride lasted about a half-hour each way, traveling on a crazy-winding road a great deal scarier than walking up the hill to Lawing. Woodland was a slightly larger wooden structure, but the facilities (or lack of them) were almost the same as at Lawing Elementary. Here I met surnames of Stowe, Sadler, Fox and Reid, particularly Ruth (for whose wedding I would play piano years later). In retrospection, I still wonder how many of those names were of relatives with mixed lineages from various plantations.

One of the joys of transferring to Woodland was the commanding appearance and friendly countenance of Mrs. Annie Roberts, the principal who was a careful, caring and astute professional. Since she taught both sixth and seventh grades in the same room, she would allow me to do some of the sixth-grade assignments in addition to my seventh-grade work whenever I would whisper to her that I had not been introduced to a certain topic. Years later, we laughed as adults when she recalled that "Sometimes I didn't know whether you were in the sixth or seventh grade." (It was uncanny that her family lived on Beatty's Ford Road leading straight to the Davidson Plantation which we ignored in those days—either through shame or disinterest.)

After completing the seventh grade in 1949, we students were then bussed on another ten-mile trip to Plato Price High, a much larger brick place containing better necessities needed for a healthier educational environment, separate buildings for elementary and junior levels, a cafeteria, band room, and choir room. My classes consisted of the usual required academics, and I also joined the chorus, directed by Mr. Paul Reid who asked if I would accompany the group in a song or two. This eager showoff-of-a-pipsqueak agreed without considering the situation seriously, for even though Mama had given permission to play hymns at the family church for free, she was surprised that I was asked to function in the role of an amateur accompanist without pay. In truth, there must have been some pride in recognizing my ability to accompany the chorus (and I did learn a great deal while improving my reading skills) but there was the unfairness of the matter, and the question on everybody's mind was why Principal McKeithan didn't hire a professional to assist the director.

After I completed the eighth grade, Mama talked with some friends while pondering what should be done since Plato Price was the only high school option for continuing rural students in that area (West Charlotte was in the city). The suggestion was made that I should apply to Lincoln Academy where Margaret Wilson was known to be an excellent musician (I didn't know then that friends like Annie Roberts were AKA sorors of Mrs. Wilson). So in 1950, Mama drove me to Lincoln Academy where Mrs. Wilson met with us and amazingly offered little thirteen-year-old me a scholarship for tuition, room and board, and "the rest is history."

NAMED IN HONOR OF ABRAHAM LINCOLN, Lincoln Academy was located in Kings Mountain, North Carolina, about forty miles south of Charlotte via Route 74. Established in 1888 by Miss Emily Prudden under the auspices of the American Missionary Association (later the United Church of Christ), it was the first school for miles around for

"Negro" children, open to the nearby community and to boarding students from afar. Set "at the foot of Crowder's Mountain" (as the opening lines of the alma mater "sang") it was actually a gradually inclining dirt road terrain rather than a steep straight-up monster of a mountain (eerily reminiscent of the hill at Lawing School) but it always made our day whenever the boys and girls were occasionally allowed to climb up the mountain, complete with proper chaperones in tow.

Lincoln served students from elementary to the senior level and functioned in at least ten buildings. There were the administration building where some classes were held, the principal's home just below the main campus, the girls' two-story wooden dormitory under matron Ma Cathey, the boys' dormitory under matron Mrs. Chavis, a cafeteria, a canteen, and elementary school buildings near the north entrance into the campus from Route 74. There was also the nearby church where we worshipped and where Mrs. Wilson was a member. Whenever we needed to shop for clothes or have our hair done on Saturdays, we were driven on the school bus to nearby Gastonia. (I didn't know then that some of my father's relatives lived there.)

My academic studies consisted of the basic mathematics, history and social science; English with the masterful Miss Jones; French under Mr. Marable (also taught math and coached the basketball team I tried to join until Mrs. Wilson forbade it in order to protect precious digits); biology with Mr. Brown; home economics with Mrs. Boulware (table manners and setting tables were easier than learning to cook and sew); and drama with Mrs. Mary Owens (who said that I exhibited good acting ability). Mrs. Margaret Wilson, the astute, all-knowing, legendary musician and mentor, and the editor of *Our African Neighbors* music booklet used in elementary schools of Gaston County, took me under her wings from the very beginning. She taught all music courses, an English class and made sure that I learned theory along with my piano studies. As director of the chorus, she trained me to accompany the ensemble, and the group sang at various sites mainly in the White community. Two outstanding students in the group were Spurgeon Webber (later trained at Meharry as a dentist) and Harold Burgess (later a medical technician in Baltimore) but I was unaware of a practical reason for bonding with either of them at so young an age.

Indubitably, Margaret Wilson was a fantastic, lifetime "Mother Mentor" of untold value. She perceived that I could use help with economics, gave me a once-a-week job tidying her home, a job as accompanist for the School Choir, a closet full of perfectly fitted clothes left behind by her daughter, Marguerite (then at Talladega from which Mrs. Wilson had graduated), and planted the notion in my head that I should also matriculate at her alma mater too. More importantly, Mrs. Wilson sought to find other support from local beauty contests (which I "nixed") to music contests, especially the awesome Sixth District Omega Psi Phi Fraternity Talent Hunt, held in various North and South Carolina cities to which she and Mr. Wilson drove me each time until I finally won first place in 1952. Among the leaders of those Omega humanists were Dr. J. A. Atkins from Winston-Salem, Drs. Dewey Duckett and W. O. Young from S.C., Mr. W. O. Yarbrough from Raleigh, and others like Mr. Reeder from Charlotte.

Concurrently, Mrs. Wilson informed me about the unbelievable information announcing Ford Foundation's four-year scholarship for Early Entrants to Fisk. Recognizing that her prayers had been answered concerning my future, she abandoned her push for the Talladega plan without hesitation and allowed Fisk to take the lead. Somehow, too, the most unbelievable miracle she performed was coaxing the Omegas to pay the remaining tuition balance after Ford Foundation's scholarship was formalized. Subsequently, Fisk sent Mrs. Minerva Johnson to our home to give me the required tests, and I passed, hence confirming the real deal. In preparation for the trip, Annie Roberts and Cousin Gwen Cunningham came to help me pack and we discussed everything an inexperienced child should need to know. Mama packed in a Bible (designed to scare me straight, especially since she added the admonition to "Stay away from the boys!").

Then, far beyond the call of duty, there were two surprises as I left Lincoln that year: Mrs. Wilson handed me a gift of $300.00 (an amount which she had saved toward Talladega's possibility and now felt that it would come in handy for the Fisk experiment) and an equally unexpected one the next year when she and principal Edgar Wilson awarded me the "missing" diploma upon my successful completion of the freshman year at Fisk in 1954.

TRAVELING TO FISK alone by train from Charlotte to Nashville, Tennessee, in the fall of 1953 caused much trepidation. I knew nothing of the other travelers, or of artifacts and histories of famous men which I would encounter at the prestigious institution. In the haste and excitement of the moment, I had done no research on Fisk. Hence, I was in for a super surprise.

While en route, pondering possibilities and trying to plan what might be, I met other Charlotte students headed to Fisk, but felt only slightly less solitary and uneasy, while they seemed so sure and frisky. In awe of everything in view, this country bumpkin knew nothing of "going it alone," getting about in a larger city of another state, or of the accompanying students seemingly more at ease than I. Struggling to contain my anxiety,

I eventually sensed that I was on my own in a place much farther from home than Kings Mountain, that I was expected to grow up fast and deal with the reality of learning new things, so I marched forth in the knowledge that enrolling at Fisk was a plus, and no matter how it was counted, here stood my future, glaring straight into my eyes.

Upon arrival at the train station, impressive male students welcomed us newcomers and served as "taxi drivers." Assisting us with luggage, they drove to the campus, finally dropping me off at Dunn House, the dignified two-story brick structure designated for us Early Entrants. There I met the wise and caring "Ma Holtzclaw" and a few other females arriving on the same day, introducing themselves as Barbara Crockett from Raleigh (assigned as my roommate), Maryann Gay (who would become my senior year roommate and Tom Rozzell's wife after graduation), Jane Fort from Nashville, Donna Penn from Evanston, Jacqueline Walton from Macon, Ellena Stone from Houston, Jeanne Johns, Gloria Marshall (destined to become Niara Sudarkasa, the first female president of Lincoln University in Pennsylvania) and others.

After settling in, we gathered in the dining room for a lovely supper scheduled in the evening, where a sharp student named Louis Garner delivered our meals. As time progressed, I timidly ventured outside and soon met some of other most interesting and talented students than one could imagine. Along the way were Alma Johnson (who would later marry Colin Powell and live in VA); Alcee Hastins (later a lawyer, judge and congressman from Florida); Richard Turner, Ruth Cooksey and Frances Hines, organ majors; the Brooks sisters from Memphis, musicians; Carol Stone and Harvey Van Buren Jr., musicians (the latter of whom won the Omega Talent Hunt before I); Preston King and David Lewis (history); Thomas Rozzell, Joseph Johnson, Lawrence Jordan (who would marry

Carol Lamar), all scientists; and Arvis Latting (a suave one from Memphis who later became a banker.

Successive walking tours revealed that the wider campus exhibited good order and well-kept grounds spread out along 16th and 17th streets north, with clear glimpses of Jefferson and Meharry boulevards just outside the fenced rock boundaries where we weren't allowed to wander without permission. The size and intimacy of the Fisk campus felt just right for someone whose comparative experience was so limited. Not too far from Dunn House was the coop (canteen) tucked into some little space "over there somewhere," which we teens would "infrequently frequent" to dance to the music of Motown Masters.

More importantly, I was awed by buildings on frontline display such as the tall, imposing brick Library, the neat Administration Building; the hugely overpowering Jubilee Hall positioned in the middle of the Oval semicircle near President Charles S. Johnson's residence (I was not aware that it was built by the "breath and sweat" of the Jubilee Singers beginning in 1871, whose tours from Nashville to other American cities and to nations abroad played a large role in saving the university from complete ruin from the Reconstruction to the early modern eras); the unique old chapel with its explosive bell tower outside, and inside, the special pipe organ positioned on the altar just under the Jubilee Singers painting gifted by the Queen of England; the Harris Music building next door, where a lot of my time would be spent in teaching studios and practice rooms; the Little Theater, where a few Early Entrants would engage in plays; and the fantastic Carl Van Vechten Gallery where the unfamiliar, but impressive art of Aaron Douglass hung. To be sure, I was overwhelmed by the historical heaviness of my surroundings and immediately developed a love for the university's worth.

In my mind's eye, my first negative impressions were that courses would be too steep, that everybody was smarter and more mature than I, that every female owned a mouton coat, and that nobody was born into rural realms and large families except me. Consequently, intimidation abounded at "first take," and I felt strongly that neither my educational nor economic status would ever match up with anything or anybody. On the contrary, the group of new acquaintances proved to be more friendly than expected, wore warm smiles, were more seriously centered on their own plans and couldn't have cared less about my status. So "shaking in my boots," I coaxed my nerves to settle down and pull myself together without unnecessary qualms and I went about pretending to be courageous and all-knowing despite the fact that I was uneasy about the unknown effect of missing an entire school year, among other fears. Fortunately, I found that Fisk had planned for missing courses like geometry and algebra to be taken far in advance of freshman requirements; thus, some of my uncertainty surceased.

Academic courses partly consisted of geometry and algebra, and dear Early Entrant James Parish occasionally served as an unofficial math tutor whenever I ran to him with a problem. Miraculously passing both courses, it still took me a while to realize my potential and develop a belief in myself enough to conquer the forthcoming subjects, such as French and German, the latter under Professor Herr Gowa who advised, "Fraülein Roach! You have first to master ENGLISH before you can speak German!" Actually, I was pretty proficient in English grammar, so had little problem WRITING translations. However, I had bungled nerves, a twisted tongue and untold fear when attempting to SPEAK foreign languages, and I was a first-rate introvert, which didn't help. Fortunately for me, another unofficial tutor, the gracious, impeccably dressed Clayton Gray who seemed to be a walking encyclopedia in ANY subject, was listening to the conversation between Dr. Gowa and me. Always a gentleman with exquisite manners, he smiled at my naivety and volunteered to help with the task of speaking German—much to the welcome relief of both Herr Gowa and me! By the time I reached philosophy and Plato's *Dialogues*, I was "good to go." Soon thereafter, I was allowed to take regular "college level" courses and was allowed into the regular four-year curriculum, after I had accumulated enough credits to become a sophomore. So being an Early Entrant didn't delay my progress into the regular upper classes. (Whoop de doo!)

The content in music courses were less scary, for I had studied music for more years than I had known German. There were History with Dr. Arthur Byler; Freshman Theory with the keen-eared Arthur Croley; Advanced Harmony and Counterpoint with "Father" John W. Work III ("Now, my friend, you KNOW you'll want to take counterpoint!"); Choir with Harry von Bergen, director, and Arthur Croley, organist, and unbelievably, I became choir president during my last two years. Each Sunday, we sang spirituals arranged mainly by Mr. Work, along with anthems and excerpts from composers such as Bach (Mass), Handel (Messiah) and Brahms (Requiem).

Among the amazing piano teachers were Matthew Kennedy, Anne Gamble Kennedy, Samuel Randlett, and Richard Stark, my assigned teacher for four years. As Mrs. Wilson had prepared me well by assigning theory, advanced standard pieces such as Liszt's "Un Sospiro," Hanon "Exercises" and Chopin "Etudes," Haydn and Beethoven Sonatas, and Bach pieces from the "Inventions" to the Preludes and Fugues WTC, Bk I., I was more at home with music. She also taught me concertos by Liszt and Mendelssohn (used for the Omega Talent shows) and Nathaniel Dett's "Juba Dance" (published music by Black composers was difficult to find).

Therefore, Mr. Stark's assignment of Grieg's "Concerto in A Minor" didn't frighten me, and he continued with compositions from Bach's Preludes and Fugues WTC, Bk. I along with works by standard composers of various eras—especially, Beethoven Sonatas and Chopin Etudes, etc.

Mr. Stark was as interested in my economic plight as was Mrs. Wilson. He kindly recommended me as once-a-week accompanist for the Joy Zibert Ballet Studio, located within easy reach from the campus, and a year after graduation, he persuaded Fisk Trustee Mrs. Margaret Rieser to grant me a scholarship to Juilliard School of Music, then located on Claremont Street in New York City. Other contributions by "the village" continued at Fisk. Invitations came from Mrs. John W. Work, who made delicious chili for us choir students; Mrs. Geraldine Fort, Jane's mom, who gave mentor-sessions to us Dunn House girls and who made delicious meals complete with those yummy yeast rolls; Dr. Robert Thorntons (Maryann's relatives; he taught math); dinner at Richard Starks'; and Mary Owen (drama teacher from Lincoln Academy, who also invited Mama to stay at her Nashville home upon my Fisk graduation). Rev. and Mrs. Egbert Cox (Katherine), representatives of the Congregational Church who had met me at Lincoln and Fisk, introduced me via mail to financial supporters Mrs. W. H. Henkle of Racine, Wisconsin; and Mrs. Adelaide P. Wicks, the kind Los Angeles humanitarian to many diverse students from here and abroad, who sent me monthly checks until I graduated from Yale. (I met her in person only once when Mama and I traveled to a Music Educators Conference in Los Angeles in the early 1980s. She insisted upon not accepting our invitation to dinner, but insisted upon taking US to dinner instead! How graciously warm she was!)

MY TEACHING CAREER BEGAN when Mr. John Work III recommended me to Tuskegee Institute as I sought work after graduation during the mid-summer of 1957. Having graduated in performance with an English minor rather than as a piano major with the more practical music education degree designed for teaching, I was restricted either to college teaching or private school jobs, or I could accept the offer to teach English on a B certificate pay. Therefore, my first mission was to learn how to teach at Tuskegee in just a few weeks. Beginning with the clear techniques of Nye and Nye for elementary level, I progressed through the various library books and began to glean how to disseminate information in a precise and understandable manner. There was no way I could afford to fail myself or others who had such a large stake in my education. Missing in the scramble of choosing music careers was the important subject of practice time for concerts, an agent, and a long-time sponsor needed for a performance career versus a more immediate job as teacher and with optional performances. Although learning to sing or to play an instrument was required in any music career, teaching was far more practical and immediate.

It was awesome to begin my very first job at the huge, well-maintained Tuskegee Institute made famous by the esteemed educator-founder Booker T. Washington and by the creative genius, scientist George Washington Carver. I fell in love with the large campus from the beginning, spread out over such vastness, complete with extensive degree programs in several divisions, and medical programs in hospitals for both human and animal care. Above all, I relished splurging at Dorothy Hall Guest Cottage dining room where students in hospitality and management courses cooked incomparable, splendiferous biscuits that melted in your mouth and bites of every imaginable thing in a dietician's list of good stuff to eat. (Given my humble origin, what did I know of "comparative eating-out places"? I soon learned!)

The legendary Dr. William Dawson, trombonist, composer, conductor and former chairman of the music department, had resigned just before I arrived, and was succeeded by Mrs. Lexine Weeks, who greeted me warmly and kept me abreast of all I was to do. She sat in observation and approval of my first sessions such as Music Fundamentals for nurses—who thought the can of Raid was funny); others assigned were piano, accompanist for both the choir (Dr. Relford Patterson, conductor) and for various vocal and instrumental students. I also performed a two-piano concert with Harvey Van Buren Jr. and a solo recital that year. Tucked onto my afternoon schedule were private lessons for public school students. One of the vocal teachers was Mrs. Ethel Hardy, a fine soprano from N.Y. with a bubbling personality and a laughing knowledge of "Shine on Harvest Moon" along with those arias. One of our guest performers was Thomas J. Flagg from Talladega, who later moved to D.C. where with his wife, Helen, became members of my church, Peoples Congregational UCC, where cousin Evelyn Davidson conducted the Chancel Choir. Other colleagues were Bettye Blackburn in English (my roommate at Mrs. Manley's apartments), Dorothy Butler (who would later transfer to D.C., to work as a rare African-American journalist at the Washington Post and would marry Sam Gilliam in art); and Dr. Eleanor Ison (a brilliant physiologist who would also move to D.C., marry Dr. H. Franklin and eventually become a dean of one of Howard's medical schools).

In general, I had been sheltered from aggravating racial incidents, and had never encountered any real serious situations. In the city of Tuskegee, I walked to work or to Mrs. William Dawson's clothing store, so I mainly stayed within the limits of the city nearest the institute. Once, as a diversion, a girlfriend offered to take Bettye and me shopping with her in the city of Montgomery, an hour away. Imagine the shock to my last nerve when we, upon entering the city, saw a huge sign which read: "Welcome to Montgomery. United Ku Klux Klan." That did it for me. I returned to Dawson's shop, never to return to Montgomery again.

The Juilliard School of Music was sponsored by a grant from Mrs. Margaret Rieser in 1958, so I requested of President Dr. William Foster a year's release from Tuskegee. A year in grand old New York City was an extraordinary experience. With its swift subways, tall buildings and soothing Hudson River running alongside Riverside Drive (where a small group of us Juilliard students were paid to sing in Riverside's church choir), the whole affair was surreal.

Juilliard, then on Claremont Avenue, was an eye opener, for as much music as I learned at Fisk these were different methods to drill musical information such as keyboard harmony, where there were oral directions to construct on-the-spot number of measures, with given harmonies, all in a certain meter and key without the use of a syllabus or text in sight (thank goodness for John Work's depth of instruction WITH the Tovey textbook which gave me solid recall); in Ear Training, we used a songbook text to sing Sol-fa syllables while simultaneously conducting the beats; foreign languages involved verbal translation from musical scores; and in Literature and Materials, we took turns playing various pieces in chronological order of standard eras instead of listening to recordings (for the classical, I did Haydn's "Sonata in E Minor" and received good applause). In previous settings, I was among the few who was rated "excellent," but at Juilliard, EVERYBODY in the crowded classroom could play with excellence. Other highlights enjoyed immensely were singing "Job" under the baton of guest conductor Leonard Bernstein, and studying piano with the fascinating Katherine Bacon, who assigned more literature than I knew existed. Among some of my assignments were Bach's "Preludes & Fugues from Well-

Tempered Clavier, Bk. II"; short Brahms exercises designed to twist the brain from ever-changing chord progressions; several Brahms "Intermezzi"; Beethoven's "Concerto in C"; and lots of Chopin, especially the "Prelude" in B-flat minor. Alas, that valuable year was over all too soon.

While in New York, I was thrilled to meet such interesting persons as student Shirley Verrett, the mezzo soprano, whom a few of us idolized enough to tag along with her as often as we could (and I "chanced" upon her again briefly when she visited friends at Yale's Norfolk summer school); pianist Arlene Saison from France; Grace Feldman, serious string player; Nathan Carter, whose graduate recital we observed him conduct (later taught at Morgan); and Dr. Kwabena Nketia, from Ghana, who visited the school while I practiced in a studio. Other personalities were Barbara Conrad whom Belafonte sponsored after Texas backlash removed her from the starring role in an opera; George and Minnie Meares (when I accompanied the N.Y. Omega program); and Marian Miller, the delightful daughter of Rev. Egbert and Katheryn Cox from California, who invited me to dinners.

Indubitably, the most important godsend living in close-by Brooklyn was my sister, Geneva, who worked at a garment factory and came to my rescue several times over, rendering monetary and other support such as drilling subway directions to Brooklyn where I could enjoy her meals (nobody seasoned chicken like she did!), raid her clothes closets, and find peace in her love. She called me "Cookie" and really spoiled me and I called her "Ginny." Indeed, we had a special bond and I regretted that my stay in N.Y. was so short, but at this crucial time, economic needs in such a big city commanded me back to work in Tuskegee and Ginny could not continue to break her budget for my dreams. So at the end of the year, I thanked Ginny, Mrs. Rieser (who was open to my continuing), and Mrs.

Bacon as I turned down her suggestions to apply to Juilliard for a scholarship and/or accept the kind offer of her purse to increase the length of my stay in order to obtain a degree. By then, however, I was centered on economics and questions about degree choices and thus returned to Tuskegee.

Within a year's time, I reflected upon my situation and requested another leave at the end of 1959 in order to pursue a master's degree, and in order to upgrade my pay. As invaluable as the Juilliard experience was, the mistaken inclusion of a course already taken at Fisk and the system unique to Juilliard which would take another year still wasn't in a master's degree program. Although Tuskegee was a comfortable place to work, I needed to pursue a graduate degree to increase my worth. Grappling with various conflicting ideas, I made a decision to apply to Yale University in New Haven, a setting in a city small enough for me to maneuver easier than at Columbia in New York. Upon acceptance at Yale, there were offers of both a scholarship and loan, and the possibility of finding practical work.

Seeking advice for additional funding was another matter. Dr. Daniel Williams, librarian, assisted me in researching funds, as did Dr. Stanley Smith, sociologist, who advised me to apply to the State of Alabama, whose Jim Crow laws prohibited me from doing graduate study in the State, but might award supplementary funds for out-of-state studies. No matter that it seemed like an insult to beg favors from someone who rejects you, I was grateful that the State of Alabama granted a positive answer. A grant from John Hay Whitney completed the tuition balance, and I was able to land at Yale during the fall of 1960. The only downside was that the program was three years and would obliterate any notion of time for close contact with friends at home. I took the chance, for my mind was set upon goals and responsibilities that didn't exactly fit in with raising children and learning sonatas simultaneously, so the "die was cast"!

UPON REACHING YALE UNIVERSITY in New Haven, Connecticut, in the fall of 1960, I found what seemed a paradise on earth. The beautiful institution with unusual landscaped grounds and impressive living structures was laid out as separate "campuses within a campus" or separate schools set apart from each other in quadrangle or various other church-like designs in a vast range of real estate. Checking into Helen Hadley Hall where graduate women who were entering Yale for the first time would live, I was greeted by the attractive, gracious director who showed me an appointed room where I would stay for the next few years. After getting settled in, I proceeded to search for my sanity and decided to look for places I would be expected to appear. The School of Music included Stoeckel Hall, Woolsey Hall and Sprague Hall and other spaces used for classes, practice or performance, all collectively becoming my "homes away from home." It took a while to walk all those blocks to wind up at the right place on time, in snow or not, and to spend the right amount of time catching up at yet another school. Meanwhile I learned that the three-year degree residency could be reduced to two and one-half years, pending study at summer school in Norfolk, Connecticut; my hope was that time would pass fast as I sought to learn more.

I was assigned to Seymour Fink, the perceptive piano professor who taught me his "stick fingers" technique to strengthen my digits, thus making production easier without undue labor (he later made a video of this unique method). A highlight of my time at Yale was winning the Lockwood Scholarship contest with Beethoven's "Waldstein Sonata"—a monetary/performance award[1] with an opportunity to play with a small orchestra under Gustav Meier's baton (pianist John Bollinger, also Fink's student, played orchestral parts for preparation before rehearsals with the orchestra). Inadequate and obscure answers were given in answer to why the awkward Shostakovish Concerto with its ragtime rhythms and uncomfortable-sounding harmonies was chosen for me while the other two contestants were assigned Mozart and Brahms, and I wondered why a concerto which I already knew such as the Grieg couldn't be used. However, time for challenging—possibly Bruce Simons, head of piano—was limited, so I dug in with a "stiff upper lip" and a pout, but I still felt a particular slight. Others of my teachers were Janet Knapp, who placed me in the Collegium Musicum group to sing my way through the madrigals and motets as a practical way to learn history; Lawrence Moss, Donald Martino and Allen Forte in theory; and the extraordinary ensemble coaches: pianist Ward Davenny, conductor Gustav Meier, cellist Aldo Parisot, clarinetist Keith Wilson and violinist Broadus Erle. Quite a bit of time was spent in chamber ensembles. I enjoyed accompanying graduate recitals such as Phil Young's bassoon recital (he gave me the complete Tovey edition of Beethoven's "Sonatas" for playing with him) and there were numerous trio and quintets by Mozart, Beethoven, Schubert and others. John Bollinger and I also performed duo pianos with the orchestra in Igor Stravinsky's Rite of Spring.

At Yale, "rubbing elbows and touching the garments" of talented African-Americans proved particularly rewarding. Some of the ladies at Helen Hadley were Ruby Purnell from Atlanta, who later served on a Yale Board after her graduation, later adding "Hearn" to her name; Amelia Cobb in drama from Washington, D.C., who later added "Gray" to her name and later became my colleague at the University of D.C.; Inez Smith (later Reid),who became a judge in D.C. and a member of my church; Eleanor Holmes, law student often observed in the Law School Dining Room, later to become a D.C. congresswoman; Marian Wright (later Edelman), law student sponsored by the Rev. William (Bill) Coffin family, who showed Mississippi's unequal plight to Robert (Bobby) Kennedy and later founded the Children's Defense Fund; and the legendary lawyer and minister "Sister" Pauli Murray, absolutely one of the most awesomely wise persons I ever met, and whose friendly chats were unbelievably full of wisdom whenever I chanced to meet her in passing, or when I occasionally interrupted her meals at the dining room (at the time, I did not know of her contributions to the 1954 Supreme Court decisions for which Thurgood Marshall et al received most of the credit; now did I know of her significance to the priesthood, or that she would be honored later to have a Yale college named in her honor). In any case, my whole soul was gladdened by her presence and by all of these marvelous women whom I was so pleased to meet.

Meanwhile, I applied for a part-time job at Helen Hadley Hall as one of the switchboard operators-receptionists, who connected residents to phone calls or buzzed their rooms to announce guests. Taking on this responsibility meant that squeezed schedules would rule out any commitment to Freedom Rides of the 60s, parties where the Chubby Checker twist was danced, and many other social events. So be it, I felt, because I simply had to honor my commitment to the scholarship rules, and I could not suffer more years being so broke. Although I usually couldn't "walk and chew gum at the same time," you better believe I was determined to do my best, because the salary would pay back the Yale loan before graduation, along with other responsibilities. So when the time to play my graduate recital neared, I walked two miles to the hotel closest to the campus, booked reservations for the Crawfords and Mama to attend the recital, and then took a bus downtown to look for a recital gown (I should have found more time to shop for a more elegant gown for the most important concert of my life). Special surprise guests who attended the recital were friends from Harvard (Jane Fort was working there and Carolyn Padelford was studying there—both erstwhile exchange students between Pomono and Fisk); and the gracious Dr. Ulysses Kay, a Yale graduate, exceptional composer, educator, and editor at BMI (whose music was recommended by Ward Davenny) came to hear me play the premiere of his Four Inventions.

After Yale, I didn't stay for graduation exercises, and my teaching career continued at Fayetteville State College for six years, where President Dr. Rudolph Jones hired me in 1962, and where both he and Dr. Mary Terry Eldridge, chairperson, became special mentors at every turn whenever I couldn't figure things out. Alongside Thomas Bacote, band director, I worked as teacher of piano, music fundamentals and accompanied the choir which Dr. Eldridge conducted. She was the best! It was she who advised me in the purchase of my first home, suitable for Mama, the piano and me. To afford expenses, I played organ church services for Rev. Thomas and Rev. Massey for a while, and adding to the "tight" after-school schedules, took upon myself 50 extra private piano students, adding an assistant, Ms. McNair, to help with the ever-flowing line of students whom I could not turn away in this quest for the pursuit of enough wealth to accommodate a house, car and the support for Mother and me. (One student, Michael Caldwell, won first place at the Omega Talent Hunt with Mozart's "Concerto in A," later studied at the N.C. School of the Arts and in Florida, served as U.S. music ambassador to the Americas, taught in VA and FL, now retired as professor emeritus.) Comes to mind that my purse could have been larger, had I known how to negotiate "relinquished" contract requested by Tuskegee.

Shortly afterwards, Harvey Van Buren Jr. took leave from Howard University in order to study organ in Belgium with Flor Peters. He asked if I would substitute for him in 1966. I requested leave from Fayetteville State and a deal was made with Dr. Warner Lawson to serve for a year. As Harvey's wife joined him, I sublet their apartment while maintaining my home in Fayetteville so that Mama could keep the studio open for my substitute to teach students I left behind. Although I liked the Fayetteville State job, I wasn't sure if I'd ever return to teach, but the option was there. And although I had made several valuable friendships, still it seems that I just HAD to see the rest of the world.

AT HOWARD UNIVERSITY, I taught piano and accompanied instrumental students, as well as some few vocal students of Carolyn Grant (including Jessye Norman). I also performed a solo recital highlighting works by African-American composers Thomas Kerr, head of keyboard, and Mark Fax, organist-composer and assistant dean, along with standard works by Beethoven et al. I was also delighted to meet in person Dr. Warner Lawson, head of Fine Arts; Cecil Cohen, pianist-composer; vocal teachers Louise Burge, Lorraine Faxio and Hilda Harris; and theorist Madeleine Coleman, among others. The most pleasant surprise of all was to finally meet a legend from my own family, cousin Evelyn Davidson White, who taught theory and also served as assistant choral director for Dr. Lawson. Mama had told me to look for her there, but I was surprised to meet her all the same. Initially I was intimidated by her celebrated status and praise that preceded her awesomely dignified presence, her professional authorships and renown. In time, she became a most precious counselor and I followed her lead to Peoples Congregational United Church of Christ, where she conducted the Chancel Choir. There I met Rev. Dr. A.

Knighton Stanley, son-in-law of Andrew Young; Thomas and Joan Stanley; Associate Minister Leslie Cannon Dowdell (Fiskite and AKA), Dr. David Driskell family (he had taught at Fisk, the University of Maryland, and also created the stained Amistad windows at Peoples); Davey Yarborough, musician; the fabulous soprano Carmen Balthrop; and Mr. Reeder, who said that he had met Grandma Caldwell in his youth when he attended Bible School at Nazareth Baptist; and Walter Robinson, an original Tuskegee airman. I enjoyed meeting Peoples' guest speakers such as James Baldwin, author-activist, and the famous Tutus from South Africa, among others. I also met special persons in whose courts Jim Stafford worked such as judges Norma Holloway and Jay Johnson and Carl Moultrie (Omega's national secretary) for whom the D.C. Superior Court was named.

As the year ended, Harvey returned to reclaim his job, but I had decided not to return to N.C. Therefore, Dr. Lawson kindly recommended me to Dr. Nathaniel Gatlin, chairman and director of band at Virginia State College. There I met teachers Willis Patterson (bass in TV premiere of Menotti's "Amahl and the Night Visitors"; Dr. Oscar Henry, magnificent tenor; Undine Moore, pianist-composer who taught theory; pianist Mr. Mamon Morrison, his student Patricia Sizer (clarinetist and AKA undergrad basileus whom I saw again when she taught in D.C. public schools). Above all, there was the marvelous pianist, Altona Trent Johns, daughter of college president William Trent, and wife of Vernon Johns, who preceded Martin Luther King at Dexter Ave. Church, and mother of Jeanne Johns, my fellow Early Entrant to Fisk. I spent one interesting year at Virginia State, teaching piano and accompanying vocal and instrumental students, and I accompanied Bernstein's "West Side Story" under Willis Patterson's direction. I also performed a solo recital including works by

Beethoven, Chopin, and African-American composers and toured as pianist in Antoinette Handy's "Trio Pro Viva."

While living in D.C., I had managed to purchase a small home in nearby Silver Spring into which I moved Mama while putting the N.C. house on the market. This overwhelming arrangement found me commuting on weekends until the end of the 1967-68 semester. Meanwhile, during the summer break of 1968, Florence Van Buren had informed me of a plan to establish a new college scheduled to open that fall in D.C., so I applied. Running into Charles Young, a former colleague from Fayetteville, I was recommended by him as a competent musician.

Federal City College (now University of the District of Columbia) was established as part appeasement to D.C. citizens after the riots that exploded in direct reactions to the assassinations of the Kennedys and Dr. King. Leaders felt that justice demanded that there should be affordable tuition rates and open enrollment. First led by Dr. Frank Farner as appointed president, he was succeeded by several other presidents and/or interims from Drs. Harland Randolph, Lisle Carter, Mr. Claude Ford, et al, to the current Dr. Ronald Mason. First situated in D.C. at Second and D Streets, N.W., its parts expanded across the city to include blocks on 10th St., N.W.; 13th and H, N.W.; New York Avenue, N.W.; North Capitol and South Dakota, N.E., etc. In 1976, the Teachers College, Washington Technical Institute and Federal City merged to become the University of the District of Columbia, whose main campus is now located at 4200 Connecticut Avenue, N.W., where the Music Department eventually settled.

When I arrived for work in the fall of 1968, my first task was to help plan core courses to determine fields of study. When it was decided that there would be a music core (and how could this not be for a majority of

Black citizens?) I worked with the administration to recruit teachers. Students wandered about giving suggestions and asking questions to unsolved problems, but we were soon in motion and key teachers were positioned in good time. Among the first hires were Robert Felder, instrumental head; George Edwards and Arthur Dawkins, woodwind; Nelda Ormond, vocal section with Anne Burt, Charlotte Hollomon (daughter of Charles Wesley), et al to follow; Dr. William Moore, pianist, music chairman and choral director (later succeeded by the current chairperson, Judith Korey (piano-theory); and pianists Hildred Roach, Drs. Marva Cooper and Percy Gregory.

In addition to standard literature, UDC became a pioneer in Black Studies in which courses were added to the curriculum such as Jazz, with Calvin Jones as trombone-director, supplemented by Steve Novosel on string-bass and percussionist Tom Teasley; Gospel, with pianist-singer Pearl Williams-Jones as head; and my research begun in 1969 led to a course with textbook for History of African-American Music. Struggling with media, music, materials, measurements and computers, I gave numerous lecture-recitals, and collected a sizable amount of scores and recordings to teach the course and also coordinated a TV video of Black composers with coworkers and students as performers. (YouTube had not developed into today's asset). Two of the grants that I received to do research were from the American Forum in 1969, which gave me the opportunity to travel to Ghana with a short stopover in Paris) and another from UDC's CARUP faculty grant, which allowed me to do summer study in the Caribbean.

Together, both standard and ethnic programs at UDC produced outstanding graduates who became mainly performers and public schoolteachers in the Metro area such as Allyn Johnson (pianist-director successor of Calvin Jones), Davey Yarborough, James Palmore, Jamal

Brown, David Cole, David Chisholm, Pete Muldoon; Anthony Moore, Eric Summers, instrumental; Johnny Butler; Raymond Jones (later earned doctorate, now president, of Cornish College); Otis Alexander, Martin Ford, Jackson Cesar, Detra Battle, earned master's at Catholic University, and received "good reviews" and Marissa Harris, et al, vocalists. Some of my piano students were Michael Green, received Lowell U. scholarship; Brett Rankin, later earned doctorate; James Logan, earned master's degree from C.U.; Venetta Bumbry (later earned master's); Henry Herrera, works in Catholic Church and school music); Maria Angelova from Bulgaria w/further study at U/Md. and Callye Christopher, from D.C., et al.

In conclusion, my entire life and career accomplishments stand as a tribute to all who came together to support my goals, for no one stands alone, and no one can conquer anything of worth without help. Indeed, without "Amazing Grace" from God, family, foundations, the Omegas, AKAs and the diverse "villagers" whom I can never repay, tasks would not have been as easy, for it took more than a notion to launch a career in the field of music. Busy from beginning to the end of my career, I seemingly always found myself in a never-ending race, even during my one-year sabbatical—not so much to compete, but to make sure I could keep up or catch up. I never felt as though I had learned everything one needs to know about music. Try as I might, I could not solve the "pressure overload" and my schedule usually felt like "on-call" duty of a preacher or a doctor, especially when I taught those fifty after-schoolers in Fayetteville, had to learn the computer (which interfered with piano practice) and researched for writing a textbook. Economics were always in competition with time. A reflective overview of my career is summarized thusly: Perhaps the most important lesson I learned the hard way was that the brain resents being abused by nonstop schedules of overwhelming overloads, all without proper rests and vacation breaks, and can quit on you when it is pressured beyond its capacity to work well. ('Nough said.)

For economic and other reasons, I tackled "dead last" the difficult but important decision to either marry or remain single, after I had earned the master's degree, purchased a house, a car and cared for Mother. (Just as in farming, it takes more time than one would think to study and cultivate a companion well enough to make a choice.) My community didn't do debutante balls and such. Besides, the fellows "next door" were all cousins, and even if I HAD been home at 16, I had not maintained contact with the cute little preteen who'd often bought me ice cream across the street from church, and neither of us had the presence of mind (or patience) to maintain connection over so many years and over so many states. Meeting briefly as adults, time and space had "done us in" and neither of us could find words to connect; he'd secured a job in Nashville, and I, one in Fayetteville, thereby placing us in the exact same position in reverse as we had been at sixteen. In another case, one of the few Black men I saw at Yale invited me to the nearby movie theater while "refraining" during the whole walk there and back about his having met the lovely Diahann Carroll some place, somehow. Clearly fate had deemed that neither of these unions would materialize. As for other possibilities, there was always this fear of new folks and their idiosyncrasies; I was not comfortable with the two or three "snap proposals" I had received, I did not want to live abroad, and I never wanted to be a preacher's wife. Hence it took a while before I could wrap my head around the idea of any serious union at all. Then one day, I ran into James Stafford by chance. He'd attended Howard Law with Carolyn Davis and Vernon Jordan, served as a JAG in the military in Colorado, and his law office was near mine in NW. We'd not seen each other since Fisk campus days when we'd wave as we passed, in the choir, or at Vespers or "wherever."

Somehow, we bonded through some "miracle remembrance" of long-ago love of Nat King Cole and Chopin (once deer peered through the window as I played his favorite Chopin) and after a while, married in the Ellicott City courthouse in 1996.

We switched from our separate places of abode to a larger Silver Spring residence and collaborated on the fun projects of becoming part-time mentors and playing roles of surrogate parents for my great nieces from Atlanta, Senetra and Charlene. Especially during summer breaks when they visited, Jim and I did SO enjoy "molding and melding their minds," driving them to Hershey, PA; taking Charlene to work at a neighborhood pizza place; and going to parks and movies. Regretfully, our marriage lasted only eight years, when he succumbed to an untimely death. Thereafter, both nieces received Hope scholarships, grew into adulthood with their own plans in mind, with Charlene attending military college and Senetra studying at Georgia Tech, earning her Master's degree in history. However, I am not without "play children," for nieces Marlene Brooks, ex-UDC alumna retired from Voice of America, and Tommyzee Tinsley, a computer science graduate of Smith and Rutgers are both in close proximity and do serve that purpose very well.

Toward the end of my career, I accompanied numerous recitals which left no time for practicing or performing solo recitals. In retracing my travels, I'd taken a boat to sit in the middle of a river observing life at Ganvie Sea Village in Dahomey; I'd watched the Ghanaians weave Kente cloth in the hills; made visits to slave ports in Puerto Rico at El Morro Castle, in Ghana at Elmina Castle and in various sites on the South Carolina/GA Sea Island coast; I'd enjoyed tracing vestiges of African music from there to Jamaica's Maroon village and other Caribe islands, and I couldn't envision other places I wanted to go solo. Therefore, pondering mortality after at least two non-life-threatening car accidents, occasional "brain fog," a few awkward misjudgments which still haunt me, a blackout and a few falls, I counted eight years in AL, VA, NC, and nearly fifty years at UDC. At that juncture, I summarized that I had received a lot, given back a lot, and had accumulated more blessings and successes than failures or faults. Grateful for that, I then retired in 2018. At first, I felt like a "fish out of water," having left without completing all of the things I had wanted to do. However, after settling down, I am at peace with my present state. What a fine roller-coaster life continues to be, with its ups and downs, hits and misses, hard and soft landings, shared joys and love of family and friends! Indeed "I wouldn't take nothing for m'journey!"

Postscript. In hindsight, I should leave to musicians a few hints to help avoid fiascos:

(1) accept no vocal contracts; (2) accept no last – minute "gigs" with inadequate time for preparation; and (3) if an adjudicator, request preview recordings, program coordinator to control pauses for assessments, adequate lighting, and seating with a full stage view.

Hildred Roach, Then and Now

Parents Howard and Pearl Roach with firstborn Harold (1916-1971) standing and Clarence (1918-1997) on Mama's lap,

Villagers: Ma Pearl, Cousin Evelyn Davidson, Grandpa Prince Roach, Adelaide Wicks, Sis Geneva, Teachers Richard Stark, Margaret Wilson, Carrie Robinson Quander, Humanists Margaret Anderson, Ed & Katherine Cox

Marva Cooper & Hildred Roach, duo-pianos @ U.of MD; Hildred, age 8; Hildred @ Peoples church; Marva & Hildred @ N.C. Central with T.J. Anderson, Hale Smith, composers; Ira Wiggins, winds & T. Holley. cellist; Trio Pro Viva w/A. Handy. fl. & Ron Lipscomb, cellist; Jim & Hildred

Africa: Boat to Ganvie Sea Village & Lorry to Ghanaian Village.
Caribbean: Water Taxi; Taxis to Jamaican Maroons; in Trinidad.

Jeanne Joyce Adkins

Miss Annetta Baugh of Beaumont, Texas, my eighth-grade mathematics teacher at Alabama State College Laboratory School in Montgomery, was a proud Fisk graduate. She approached my mother one day and announced that she wanted me and my sister Enid to accompany her to Tuskegee University to take an exam sponsored by the Ford Foundation. We would not discover all of the details and ramifications until we arrived on Tuskegee's campus and met the distinguished poet and Fisk librarian Dr. Arna Bontemps, a very handsome and impressive figure.

Sometime later we were informed that we had passed the exam and would have the opportunity to attend Fisk University in the Early Entrants Program. Since there were two of us in the same family, it was suggested that Enid, who is 15 months older, would go first and I would wait a year to enter. As my parents had six children to educate, they did not ask our opinions but felt we were fortunate to have this opportunity. They thanked Miss Baugh and informed us that we were future Fiskites.

The following year we moved from Montgomery to the campus of Virginia State University in Petersburg, VA. Busily adjusting to a new town, new school and new friends, I hardly thought about anything else. I knew that Enid was happy in Nashville, but since I still had considerable time before departing for Fisk, I kept concentrating on the present and enjoying my days at Peabody High School. The year passed quickly; I got invited to my first prom and it was soon time to bid Virginia adieu. My parents called the high school principal, told him I would not be returning in the fall and why, and prepared for my departure.

I knew a bit about the great legacy of Fisk University and the Jubilee Singers, and that I was going to a very prestigious campus. I also knew that many Fisk students were not financially deprived and wondered if my meager wardrobe would hold me in good stead. It would not, I quickly learned, when I walked to Jubilee Hall to claim my one footlocker. There I met a fellow Early Entrant, jovial Jackie Walton of Macon, GA. Her large collection of trunks and luggage quickly confirmed my feelings of inadequacy. However, that first introduction to college life was the beginning of special friendships and lifetime bonds.

Life at Fisk our first year centered around Dunn House, our headquarters for adjusting to college life as Early Entrants. We were a wee bit jealous of the Early Entrant boys, who were housed in a more modern dorm nearby. Although we took classes together, our friendships were mostly girls with girls and boys with boys. Mother Holtzclaw, our guardian, was kind and welcoming but insisted that we mind our Ps and Qs. I was pleasantly surprised to find that a former Montgomery friend, Carol Pindle, was in our group. Those in the regular student body tended to watch us closely but I recall no issues relative to us being on campus at such a young age. Another Dunn House sister, Ellena Stone of Houston, and I had older sisters at Fisk, which provided us additional feelings of security.

Along with this sense of security came many fond memories that forever remain—Quiet Hour and other chapel events; being invited by Donna Penn to spend part of my first college summer with her family in Evanston, IL; my years being taught by the brilliant and eccentric Robert Hayden. His classes were always life-changing experiences! Through it all, our Dunn House bond remains strong even today. I can say this unequivocally, for at a recent reunion hosted by Donna at her home on Kent Island, MD, it was as if we had picked up right where we had left off all those years ago. If our paths cross again, I'm sure it will still be the same.

My life since Fisk has been interesting and diverse. I moved to Washington, D.C., and worked as an editor and Dictaphone transcriber at the U.S. Commerce Department. Two years later, I started working for the D.C. Public Library System. I had just received an offer from Countee Cullen at Howard University to work on a master's degree but I chose to marry instead. Although that marriage produced Allison, the first of my two daughters, it was one of short duration. (We are all entitled to one mistake.)

I began to tire of the hectic D.C. pace and returned to Petersburg to take a job teaching fifth grade. I also bought a small house near my parents. This move back home would play a very large part in my future. Aldrich Wendell Adkins, a colleague and dear friend of my mother's in the music department at Virginia State University (where she also had the joy of teaching with my Dunn House sister Hildred Roach), was a native of Alexandria, VA, whose father pastored Alfred Street Baptist Church there for 43 years. Aldrich was the VSU choir director and chair of the voice department. One day my porch light needed replacing and my mother asked him to fix it. While there, he also invited me to a Richmond Symphony concert. As they say, the rest is history. He and I married the following year.

It is interesting how life comes full circle. After 30 years of marriage living in Iowa City, Iowa; Austin, Texas; Atlanta; and Baton Rouge, LA, where my second daughter Amy was born, my husband retired from Southern University there. Two months after his retirement, VSU called and asked him to return as Eminent Scholar. I was offered a job writing for the college president.

I have been blessed to have Black history legacies on both sides of my family tree. My father, Vernon Johns, spent his entire life fighting for civil rights. In 1994, ABC aired a TV movie about his life, *The Vernon Johns Story*, starring James Earl Jones. Also in 1994, the State of Virginia erected a historical marker about him near his gravesite in Darlington Heights. My first cousin, Barbara Rose Johns, was a key figure in the Brown vs. Board of Education case. There is both a monument and a state office building in Richmond celebrating Barbara, and a statue of her will replace the statue of Robert E. Lee in the U.S. Capitol. My mother's father, William Johnson Trent, was one of the founders of the United Negro College Fund and served as president of Livingstone College in Salisbury, N.C., for 27 years.

I have more time now to reminisce about Fisk and all that it meant to my development. Being on a small HBCU campus where we were names and not numbers was a wonderful experience, as well as having the opportunity to meet many people from many different backgrounds and to be taught by such world-renowned professors. I am especially pleased that Fisk is now beginning to recapture its former reputation and stature. All of our life experiences make us who we are. This is especially true of the years I spent at Fisk—MAJESTIC DEAR OLD GOLD AND BLUE!

THEN (Jeanne at age 15)

NOW (Jeanne at age 60)

Jeanne's parents, Vernon and Altona Johns

Jeanne, front left, at age 6 with her siblings

Jeanne's 65th birthday luncheon,
B. Smith's restaurant, Washington, D.C.
Jeanne and Hildred Standing;
Donna and Jackie Sitting

Jeanne and Dunn House sisters at the home of Donna Towns, Kent Island, MD

Jeanne, far right, at Fisk graduation

Jeanne and late husband,
Dr. Aldrich W. Adkins

Jeanne at Virginia State
University, Petersburg, VA

Jeanne and sister Enid Johns at dedication
of Vernon Johns School, Petersburg, Va.

Barbara Laverne Crockett Dease

WHEN: Beginning 1953-1956—The Rest of My Life

WHERE: From Raleigh, NC, to Nashville, TN, to FISK UNIVERSITY (The other locations will be identified in chronological order.)

WHY: In pursuit of the best college education within my parents' grasp

HOW: In answer to a summons by the Ford Foundation

So, there I was, at the end of my sophomore high school year, looking forward to nothing more than a hot summer of hanging out with my friends. When, lo, I was given a test and the result was simply that I was ready for a special kind of education with other kids my age at the illustrious FISK UNIVERSITY—a Black college that EVERYBODY had heard of. And my Daddy and Mama wanted me to go! My brother two years younger than I had also taken and passed the test, but he was not to go, not at his age (13)—it turns out that God had other plans for him!

FALL 1953 - SPRING 1954: I found myself in September of 1953 with my trunk and suitcases entering Dunn House, the living quarters for "The

Dunn House Girls," or the BC students, or the Early Entrants, as the campus critters called us. There were twelve of us BC students in that dormitory and we found that we were separated from the rest of the freshmen because of the notion that Jubilee Hall was too grown-up for us. (They were right, but that was a hindsight observation.) For me anyway, because I was so young and naïve that I had yet to wear hosiery of any kind! My 16th birthday (occurring during my first week there) was celebrated by wearing a pair of stockings all that day. I accepted our House Matron, Mother Holtzclaw, as a foster mother without a problem.

Thus, Dunn House and Fisk University were synonymous to me—they both exposed me to a whole new life, mixed with educational and social firsts almost every day, at least for the first semester. Aside from changing my major from Piano & Music to PreMed (Daddy told me I would be a GOOD doctor), and then flunking Zoology in the second semester because I couldn't dissect a frog (!), it was a good first year for me. As a reaction to these two bumps in the road, I began to hang out with students who generally had majors based in the Liberal Arts. I found the French Club, the Stagecrafters, an excellent Dramatics Club, other subject-based clubs and—LO AND BEHOLD—the sororities and fraternities and their "secrets." With this new freedom to explore a possible major, and new and forever friends to bolster my ego, I found that I actually liked learning, and French was looking better and better to be IT. My overriding memory of that year was the freedom we had, even with the stringent parental rules that eagle-eyed Mother Holtzclaw imposed and that we had to follow as dwellers of Dunn House.

(In the long run, though, the latter observation should not have been like that, because those years were those years were just before the time in real life when Dianne Nash and John Lewis (future congressman), other famous black leaders, and many college students were walking up and down the streets of Nashville in their civil rights protest. Dangerous times off the campus in the Black neighborhoods. Security and carefree livin' on the campus. I'm sure the atmosphere was very different at Tennessee State, because most of the Nashville protesters came from there. I cannot explain our blindness or ignorance of life around us, but very few of us remember much or anything about those activities. Nor did the next year change much from what I have already stated.)

FALL 1954 - SPRING 1955: The next year was more of the same. I had become more aware of myself as an individual, as had the others evidently. There were many nighttime discussions about Good and Bad, and Intelligent, and conscientious, and religious, and smoking (evidently that was not on the No-No List because too many of us got bit, and it was not something we were worried about), and boyfriends versus friendboys, and marriage (the true rumor was that most of the Fisk girls were sent there because Meharry Medical School [men!] was right across the street and full of eligible men from lah-de-dah family backgrounds. Not a whole lot of talk about future careers because we would more than likely become wives, teachers, nurses, or the like. For a while, I was obsessed with joining the Peace Corps as an option, but Mama and Daddy had hissy-fits and a stern no to that—their daughter couldn't go abroad, it was too far away from home! I finally spared us the misery and locked into the French Major program, with English, Education and Liberal Arts courses filling up the elective options.

You know, it's so funny! But I don't remember being swept off my feet by a guy. There were plenty to swoon at, after all. We in Dunn House were strongly encouraged to do group-dating (??). Simple concept: The guys let us go with them to games, movies, etc.; we allowed them to accompany us because they provided good company and security. Obviously, this ended up with about four or five girls selecting their mates, and marrying them in the future, but still hanging around with the group for comfort. The rest of us could go out with whomever. Not one of us Dunn House girls got pregnant early, or had hurried marriages. Our biggest worry was what would happen if we got caught off-campus, or in an inebriated state, or in scary circumstances, or dated a really grown m-a-n! Meharry men didn't count in this, they were something like brothers. In fact, most of our boyfriends were just Big Brothers, and I think they thought of us as their Little Sisters.

I found myself immersed in the Stagecrafters, the drama guild and a really good one with a dynamic advisor; also in the French Club, because of the instructor's personality, and in the English Club, for the same reason. As a matter of course, and with hardly any negative mumbling, we were herded to all the cultural events and lectures by famous names—it was less hassle. So Fall and Spring Semester went by in a blur of involvement (in nothing really) and ignorance, a form of selfishness, I suppose. But my interest in Literature evolved (and has remained so all my life), maybe because having left high school before Junior Year I had not had the opportunity to become immersed in Literature. So a lot of us were getting our first exposure to it.

FALL 1955 - SPRING 1956: The previous second semester, we had made our choice of sororities and, having been accepted into Alpha Kappa Alpha Sorority, I had started the semester as Number 3 on the Fisk Ivy Line. Alas, I do not remember my Line Name or even if we really had one. This period of pledging would last from Spring 1955 to End of Fall 1955, not including the summer months, unless you haplessly landed in a job where there was an AKA. Every month was a new challenge, and never were we more thankful for our Dunn House Sisterhood to watch our backs. The majority of those who pledged from Dunn House had chosen and been accepted by Alpha Kappa Alpha, so we had plenty of company to share whatever we thought was going on, real or perceived. The Greek World exists in a world of its own. In more ways than one, it completed a Black College Education. We learned more highs and lows, more goods and bads, more about the human personality, more about individual thresholds, more about making choices, more about self-determination, more about Greek Black History (but still that outer world off-campus did not touch us) than any other kind of education could have given us. In a better-us-than-them attitude, we learned to stick with the others on line from the other Greek organizations. We helped each other a lot! We learned how to give and take and not take-take like spoiled brats. I let go of what little self-doubt I had and threw myself into the Greek World (which has really lasted from then until now). And so I became a member of Fisk University's historic Pi Chapter, located in the South Eastern Region of Alpha Kappa Alpha Sorority, Incorporated, on December 3, 1955.

The second semester of Spring 1956 was a time of remaining on our Greek elite high and being a member of a sorority (rated by others as Best on Campus), or digging in to our major subjects to make up time (and knowledge) lost before. I was doing some of both. We had been moved from Dunn House to (can't remember the name of the dorm). This Spring Semester was one of being immersed. I admitted to being partly a social butterfly, I loved Literature, and French was my springboard into the world of brain-feeding. I loved playing with words and their meanings; I loved writing and seeing what power the written word held. After this semester, it would be about eleven years before I allowed this part of me take over again.

I was also carrying a big secret: Daddy was poised to transfer me to the HBCU, North Carolina Central University, situated in Durham, about 20 miles from Raleigh, my hometown. He declared that I was not working on any of my goals by being at Fisk. (I think to this day that they were more his goals for me than mine: becoming a famous pianist, or majoring in PreMed and becoming a doctor, or catching and marrying a doctor from Meharry.) Anyway, I led the life of a former Dunn Houser cum Fiskite, and told no one, hoping that I could change Daddy's mind over a summer with constant pressuring. It didn't happen! I cried many a tear (tantrums never did work with my daddy), engaged in many a conversation (convincing at least to me). Nothing worked. He made sure I knew it was not a money concern. He just wanted me closer to home. And That Was That! And I didn't feel flattered!

But don't get me wrong! My Daddy was a Good Daddy, and I loved him so much. It took living with them to see through the Bluff and Gruff. And most of the time he was right. He took the time to see that we all got what he and Mama thought was right. And Yes, we, his children, received the same kind of punishment that the students at the school received. He had a strong personality but Mama had her way of making him human when needed. After a few jobs held before Bro (my oldest brother) came along, he and Mama decided to try for a really good job. Daddy got the job as Principal of the North Carolina School for the Blind and Deaf, which he held for twenty-seven years. Mama got her dream job of teaching High School English for the Blind. They made the job a life for all of us, who now included me, my brothers, Manuel Houston, and William Charles Crockett. We lived in a nice house on the campus, and the whole 100+ acres and a farm was our playground. We declared that all of our playmates became our friends because they wanted a ticket to Paradise, even if they had to walk down the railroad track to get there (and that included my beaux and the brothers' girlfriends).

Really, though, I had a dream of a childhood. I had wonderful teachers, caring and fun-loving friends, a traditional (for Raleigh and its Black middle class) social life, and a passel full of kinfolk stretched from Rich Square on the East Coast to Raleigh to Hendersonville in the Great Smoky Mountains. So my break to attend Fisk University was a real break from a lot of things that made up a comfortably disciplined life. My grandfather on my mother's side was the founder of the Rich Square Institute for Negro (or Colored—can't remember!) Children. His wife, Grandma Susie, was the rock of the house. The school outlasted him and almost his son, who took over his father's position. None of these educational beginnings impressed me. I played with all the cousins. By the way, I was the first granddaughter and no more girls were born until I was 12 or 13 years old, so you know I grew up as Tomboy #1. That was on Mama's side. Daddy was 6th of ten children, and since we saw less of them, we didn't know them as well. I grew up as Miss Princess because everybody thought I was a spoiled brat.

FALL 1956 - SUMMER 1958: CHEZ NCCU: I was a transfer student from the illustrious Fisk University—O, how the Mighty have fallen! Somehow, having a superiority complex never entered my mind. I do know that I knew more subject-wise than most of my peers. However, there were plenty of defects in me if they were really looking for any. On the other hand, the seeds that sprouted at Fisk were my mainstay at NCCU.

I immediately affiliated with Alpha Psi Chapter of AKA, enrolled in 3rd-year French classes, declared Education and English Literature as my minors, started German classes, and last but not least, joined the NCCU

Choir as an alto. My love was more with the choir than with AKA, simply because of the off-campus opportunities that came with being in the choir. I began enjoying this new environment and stopped mourning for Fisk. Two experiences stand out: First, I renewed friendship with two of my homeboys, both of whom weighed over 275 pounds each, and who were famous members of the NCCU football team. In those days, students got together and made up halftime entertainment, especially for basketball games. I weighed all of 90 lbs. soaking wet, as they say. They persuaded me to do a routine where I would be the ball and the rest would be up to the two of them. It drew a lot of laughs and gasps, and was popular only because the audience would never see the same routine twice—they were easy to make up. So there went my anonymity and my dependence on my Fisk reputation.

The other incident was far more serious. There was this famous Professor of English who was also the Chair of the Department of English. I had had excellent English teachers all way up: home (Mama was a high school English teacher), the Raleigh Catholic and Public schools, and Fisk, and I knew my grammar! This professor was famous in the College Language Association, had written a (or some) book(s), and had a very sensitive/touchy ego because of his eyesight. I was in an Advanced English Grammar course taught by him. My final grade was a B. When I went to see him about the grade, I presented him with all of my tests, exercises, midterm and final papers. With a shocked look on his face, he said, "You kept all of that?" He would not tell me how I had earned that grade, nor would he consider changing my grade. And he boasted that no administrator would touch any of his grades. I went home to cry on Mama's shoulder. Daddy got wind of what had happened and immediately told me we were going back to Durham to see this one-eyed man. (During the semester I had told my parents about him, and since they both were in the business of educating the blind and deaf children of North Carolina, they must have discussed this teacher.) When I saw Daddy come to the car carrying his shotgun, I told him I would take the B and be finished with NCCU. I would still graduate at least magna cum laude. And I didn't necessarily need him for a letter of recommendation, so it was okay. He drove to Durham blowing like a bull and mumbling to himself. I was very scared, because I knew he could shoot that gun and that he had a temper (kept under wraps most of the time). We found the professor, and Daddy played the waiting game—you speak first so I can decide on my strategy. It worked! The professor must have summed him up as a worthy opponent, and he told me that he had found an error that one of his student assistants had made while grading my final, and had recalculated my grade. I had just squeaked up to an A- and, in fact, he was just on his way to the registrar's office to correct the error and change the grade. He also congratulated me on the fellowship I had received to work on my Master's degree in French Education at Atlanta University. I had not been told this piece of news, so, on our trip back to Raleigh, I had to listen to Daddy gloating about how right he had been to pull me from Fisk. I would not have done so well had I stayed, and so on ad nauseam. Nor did I dare say that I would not have had this man as an instructor if.... To this day I wonder if Daddy would have threatened—or more—with the shotgun. I'll never know. The next year when I came home from Atlanta, the grapevine told me that people had noticed a definite change in the professor's demeanor and everyone was trying to figure out why.

SEPTEMBER 1958 – SPRING 1963: AT ATLANTA UNIVERSITY: Two years flew by for a lot of reasons. My major professor took a liking to my approach to "learning" (I was more of a traditionalist than most of the grad students. Besides, he reminded me so much of my Fisk French major advisor.) My dormitory (Bumstead Hall) was a great place to learn firsthand about Atlanta Black society and politics. My roommate and others were fun-loving staffers who taught me about where to hang out or not. The late fifties and early sixties in Atlanta was The Place To Be. Also, I became enamored by AU Center's Robert Woodruff Library and its Black and African collections. Again, the Fisk training came to my rescue, because it was there that Professor Arna Bontemps drummed into our brains how to do meaningful research. His examples would most likely come from Black art.

I finished my Master's degree in French Education in August of 1960, at the same period my boyfriend and I began to be serious. (More about that later!) Indeed, my life was just rolling along. In September 1960—voilà!—I was a full-time instructor of French at Clark College, one of the HBCUs in the famous Atlanta University Center. I didn't even have to look for a new apartment or roommate. My first year of teaching was spent convincing my students that I was a teacher, one who knew her stuff in spite of her 5'1" 90-pound frame and her obvious youth. I had to pull up some courage from somewhere, because, for my first class, I walked into an overcrowded classroom full of 220+-pound men. The women were there to see how I handled myself. Somehow, the grapevine had broadcast that there was a new young very tiny girl who could probably be snowed over, and French was a required course. And so they got the registration system to enroll all the athletes in my classes. I don't remember what I (or somebody—probably my NCCU major advisor who had taken a job at

Clark—"Karma") did, but it was all straightened out, and I could stop hyperventilating before each class.

Now, about my husband, William King "Billy" Dease, from Jackson, Mississippi, and a computer analyst (then) for Atlanta University. He was just out of the Army when I met him, and was returning to Atlanta to finish his BA, and walked into this job. He was very popular with the ladies and an all-around guy. We didn't even have time to stop referring to each other as boyfriend and girlfriend before we got married. We were crazy enough to set a wedding date for Easter Saturday of 1960. Crazy because we had no time for a honeymoon, not even Easter Monday, though we both needed some time off badly. Crazy because we didn't really know what we were doing! But with Mama's friends and contacts in Raleigh, they seemed to be making it happen, and Big-Time! They continually told us to do our jobs "down there" and leave everything to them up in N.C. Even my wedding gown was designed and made with only one fitting. Mama's team came together, and people said it was the most beautiful wedding held in Raleigh up to that time. It poured down on The Day, but no one seemed gloomy.

We returned to Atlanta, and someone had found an apartment on the top floor of a newly constructed Clark College dormitory, and we lived and entertained as only The Young can do. We fit easily into a group of AUC and church couples and had a good beginning of a new life. I had met quite a few Fiskites in Atlanta, because Atlanta was a city with promising futures for Black people, and Atlanta's Black decision-makers could evidently find readily available jobs for these bright people.

Clark College had found something else for me to do—be the graduate advisor for Alpha Pi Chapter of AKA. And that is where I found the other part of me that was waiting to be developed. I was still very close to my students in age, but I made sure that that did not present a problem. For some reason, the Sorors liked me, and I had some brilliant service-conscious ladies who were very popular and took advantage of their reputation to be elected or appointed to prominent positions in the Student Government Association and other student clubs. As an example, the last line that I supervised had a young lady, Miss Linda White from Chicago, who was elected Miss Clark College and who, about forty years later, would be elected as the Supreme (International) President of AKA! I was one Proud Advisor cum Mama when that happened. I attended that Boule and became famous as the Graduate Advisor to the International President, Soror Linda White in 2004 (and incidentally also to the International Treasurer too, Soror Bernadette Greer, in the nineties)!

So, we had very little money. Neither the AU Center nor Clark paid much, even though we managed to have a full life, individually and as a couple, Billy went job-hunting to provide for his family. He found one at, of all places, the Boeing Company in Seattle, Washington. Way across the United States—and me pregnant!!! Yes, pregnant and being spoiled outrageously by my Atlanta community! Billy had to report to his new job in January 1962, so I surrendered to the caring hands more than usually. Mama and I had some good cries together over the phone—after all, my baby would be their first grandchild and the first Creecy grandgirl to all. For the Crocketts, I was just another grand-something. (The Sorors of Alpha Pi believe to this day that the laying-on of so many AKA hands during my pregnancy was the reason that I am blessed with seven grandgirls, three of whom are already AKAs.)

Here's how it went: I continued my job at Clark until the end of that semester. Linda became my self-appointed driver and caretaker. She and the other ladies packed up my belongings, helped me with the business of closing down my Atlanta life, and held a goodbye party for me. Then Linda drove me and my stuff to Raleigh, NC. After a tearful goodbye, my brother Manuel drove me and my junk all the way to Seattle in my Chevy Corvair, which I gave to him after it was determined that one car was enough for this family.

I gave birth to Mitzi Elayne Dease on August 8, 1962. Luckily, I didn't have a job, because Mitzi was a "colic" baby and required a lot of A.M.-P.M. time for about four months. When I recuperated and she had calmed down, I found a job teaching Advanced French at a fairly "elite-ist" public middle school, whose name I cannot remember for anything. Looking back on my life, this was the worst job of my career. The school was full of spoiled upper-class mostly White kids at just the right age to poke fun at their new teacher, not just because she was African-American, not because she was their first Black teacher, not just because she didn't know as much Conversational French (most of them had already spent extended time in France), but ... just because I didn't know their kind of life, nor they mine. Nor, from my short period at the school, did I want to know!

So, when Billy received an invitation from Jackson State College in Jackson, MS, to come back home to start up a computer center for Jackson State, and when he found out that the same college had an opening for a full-time French professor, we both jumped at the chance to go back down South to the land of grits and catfish. And just like that, we gladly left Seattle in late July by car again.

This time, we took our time because we didn't have to be in Jackson until late August. On the way, we stopped at my husband's brother's home in Muskegon, Michigan, for a break. I am happy we did, because it was there that our bubble burst and we saw a Mississippi that we had not paid much attention to on television, the state that we would call home for the near future.

We focused our attention on the Civil Rights Movement, heard the names of its leaders and wondered how it would affect our soon-to-be adopted home. It was there in Muskegon that we witnessed the whole TV coverage of the March on Washington that was occurring at that very time. We saw the unity and we heard the dynamic speech, "I Have a Dream," by Rev. Dr. Martin Luther King Jr. Everybody who knew of us and our relocation was full of advice, most of it was to walk out of the job in Jackson and find another location. I equate the time between the Clark job and the Jackson trip back to the same bubble that I was in at Fisk University when my world was made up of my family and close friends. I could close out whatever I didn't want to acknowledge or be involved in.

Billy and I talked endlessly about what could happen in a state with rules that I had never heard of. Though Billy had been raised in Jackson, it was in a time when there was only one set of rules—"Theirs!" And his family stayed low, and lived their own lives. But I was raised where there was one environment, an all-Black one, one that didn't infringe on our everyday living. I had a race-free childhood, protected by my Daddy and his circle of friends whose job, it seemed, was to make a happy playing field for us three children and the children of our family's friends. I look back now and realize that my family was one of about twenty that made up the Black "upper-class" of Raleigh. We had our own doctors and dentists, insurance companies, Greek-letter organizations, the Links, and Jack and Jill, a pharmacy, funeral homes, a bank, a movie theatre, a newspaper, restaurants, a full-service hotel (Billy's family, when they came up for our wedding, couldn't get over staying in a Black-owned hotel! And they had no complaints!), hospitals, all the way up to our own country club! We had a truly bourgie upbringing.

So! Indeed!!! What kind of environment was I going to, and what effect would it have on the three of us? My first memory was of Mitzi's behavior. She had been a model traveler on the trip thus far. Then, the moment we crossed the state line from Tennessee to Mississippi, she threw up all over, cried while we cleaned up, and didn't stop crying until we were almost in Jackson. Some welcome! Did our baby sense something that we didn't and react to it? No immediate answer.

SEPTEMBER 1963 - AUGUST 1973. AT JACKSON STATE: We settled into a unit of the Faculty Apartments. This was in August of 1963. There I was on a campus again, in the classroom, teaching French to very sweet ambitious boys and girls on the cusp of adulthood. I was still very close to the students in age, and I had a baby girl that they could love on and pamper as much as they wanted to. In this way, I was allowed to spend chunks of time working on projects that enhanced my future development in French, Foreign Languages, and the Humanities, and solidify my reputation as a workaholic. Too, this campus became my bubble and allowed me to help others prepare their bubbles of safety. The Freedom Riders, SNIC, and Civil Rights Protesters and other organizers were in town, for Black Jackson opened its churches, its privately owned buildings, and such, to give the leaders room to establish their programs in Civil Rights Defense.

Within this mutual bubble, I found that we were very welcome into the Greek family, specifically Alpha Kappa Alpha, Inc.–Beta Delta Omega Chapter in the city, and Gamma Rho Chapter at Jackson State, and Billy to Alpha Phi Alpha, Inc., in the city and Delta Phi on campus. I became the graduate advisor to Gamma Rho, and that lasted until 1973, then again from 1977 to 1985 or '86. As the graduate advisor, I supervised the chapter's yearly program, kept them hooked up with the South Eastern Region and its chapters, and the international meetings. Many people thought that being a grad advisor was fun and superficial, but it is hard work. Compare it to being the mother figure to many girls who depended on her. All of these years I had my own mother figures to turn to, starting with my own mother, so I knew what a difficult role it would be.

The one thing that disturbed my progress was that, in 1966, I had a still-birth, another girl. That rocked my boat. It wasn't so much the leave of absence that was forced on me. Rather, it was my recognition that I was human and that bad or unexpected things could happen to me. My Fisk/Dunn House "alter-education" had bolstered my self-confidence and had made me acknowledge both the positive and negative sides of things.

Two other unexpected events came along to shake my tranquil bubble. I became pregnant once again, this time it was a boy, William K. (Billy K.) Dease II. We almost lost him because his umbilical cord was wrapped around his little neck, but he was so determined to stay here on earth that he fought that cord and remained with us. Second, we were ending the 1969-1970 school year when the Jackson Police (all White men) moved "to quell" the Black/White unrest on JSU's campus. They shot up the F. O. Alexander Women's Dormitory, killing two men who were walking on the campus. I was five months pregnant with Billy K., and I had just left the campus to go home (we had bought a house by then), when the police invaded the campus, so I was not there. Good thing, though—mothers and fathers and everybody's uncle too called my husband and me to get word or news of their child(ren) on campus. Because of that, all events for the rest of the year were cancelled. Students were told to go home. No graduation, no nothing! Except that all that summer, parents called asking for the latest news. Since I went immediately on maternity leave, I missed all the summer meetings and other events. Billy K. was born on September 30, 1970. This time my bubble was not so tranquil. But I used the time to read up on Mississippi, my adopted home-state, and how we were still suffering from racist treatments, and how knowledge of the humanities could put another face to one's civic education and community responsibilities.

My academic life was evolving as well. Every bit of the Liberal Arts environment pulled on me to continue building my connections and research. Without Fisk's choices of instructors, lectures, programs and extracurricular activities for the BC College kids, I wouldn't have known how to make proper use of all the enrichments that I had to translate into actual use. For instance, students were asking questions that sent us all to the Library because our generation had taught them to ask and ask until they got some kind of satisfactory answer. The time was now to make good on our promises. And my boss was there to tell me truths like I had really earned my salary so far, but there would come a time when I regretted the time I was losing.

My academic vice president constantly encouraged me to look at continuing on to a doctoral program. He took me along to many events where I would meet "the right people." He reminded me that I was nearing the pay increase period when my yearly raises would be little or nothing. He informed me that Mississippi had a law made for people like me—State funds would pay most of the total cost of the degree, but I would have to pursue a degree or field of study that was not offered by the three White universities. Still sounded good to me because at that time Mississippi universities did not even offer a Master of Arts degree in French, French Education, Foreign Languages, or any mixture of the three. Then, he brought my attention to a dynamic doctoral program at the Florida State

University in Tallahassee, FL, which had a wonderful program for the Ph.D. Degree in French. It was about five hours from Jackson, yada-yada! The only request I made was that the degree would NOT be in French Education or some hybrid degree, but in French Literary Studies or some sort of French Literature.

1973 – 1976: FLORIDA STATE UNIVERSITY: All arrangements were made for my family. At three years of age, Billy K. was too young to stay with his Daddy. Mitzi at 11 years was in that awkward age where she didn't want any changes. Looked at like that, there was no choice. Both children would come with me to Florida for at least the first year, then we would evaluate the results. Thanks to members of the local Jack and Jill Chapter, we found an apartment near the campus. The FSU Foreign Language staff helped to get Mitzi into a good public school and Billy K. into a Tallahassee Public Schools kindergarten. The next year Mitzi would attend the FSU Laboratory School (the best that Tallahassee had to offer). My first year in school in fifteen years was very trying. I took three graduate courses and taught two classes, one of them at night, and managed to take care of my family of three. When I taught at night, my next-door neighbors would be happy to babysit Billy K. It Really Does Take a Village! All was well with the Dease Family. Billy drove to Florida periodically to check in with his absentee family. The second year, I sent Billy to his Daddy, and Mitzi stayed with me, a man with a four-year-old boy and a woman with a teenage girl.

These years affected Mitzi and Billy K. quite a lot. She was well on her way to becoming a spoiled princess, until I made her learn to cook and clean up, and do all the menial chores, because I would have a horrific schedule, sometimes teaching day as well as night classes. At home in Jackson, most of these chores fell on my shoulders, because she was busy doing only what interested her and being a social butterfly. Billy K., on the other hand, was busy being Mr. Dease #2, which meant following him to church, football and basketball games, becoming a favorite with the team members, and worrying his teachers to death! Since his Daddy was JSU's game announcer, everyone expected him to be with him. Daddy Billy became the "Father of the Years" since he was seen doing all that his absent wife wasn't there to do. And those things he couldn't do, he'd make a telephone call and there was always a sympathetic mother who helped out. He and Billy K. made friends with the JSU Dining Hall Staff and found that they would be happy to give them two meals anytime he asked. At the end of two and a half years, we packed our stuff and I moved back home, only to have a recalcitrant Billy K. standing in the door to point out what was his and his Daddy's and what was mine and Mitzi's. He had become a Daddy's Boy big-time and there was no room for Mitzi or me. It took all kinds of psychological effort and a couple of years to change his mindset about who belonged to whom. I have thanked the Good Lord many a time for the friends we had at JSU who took care of my family while I was gone.

As for me and the program, I was learning the tricks of the trade. I was the only Black to enroll in their many programs. But it didn't mean much because I was in a program that had many di-ver-si-ties (even though none of us knew that word then, or how much it would affect us post-FSU). I learned that professors got big bonuses for at least three things. The first was if a professor was responsible for an undergrad student becoming a major in one of the many programs which fell under the umbrella. Second was if a professor's student major continued with one of the many graduate programs. And third was when that professor's student got or had a job already before graduation. (That was why all the French professors were courting me—I already had a solid job.) Departmental money was spent sending students to where the job was, and incidentally if the student landed a job. So my second semester, I was often treated to dinner, or extended an offer to accompany a teacher to campus meetings, or the like. I was a "double-bonus"—French was going to be my major and I would go back to JSU with a job as department chair, rank of Associate Professor of Modern Foreign Languages. So, unbeknownst to me, somehow all of this was known, and I was trudging along, knowing nothing.

The most interesting thing was that all I knew was that I was being treated mighty nicely! But we all were to some degree. The other plum up my sleeve was I had to choose a major professor. Old French/Williams; 17th Century/Mrs. Allaire; 18th Century/Mr. Allaire; 19th Century/Cancalon (the lady with a baby who somehow could make all of us have a headache every day!) or Carrabino; 20th Century/Carrabino. Since I had to have a specialty, I really did like Old French, which was a surprise to me. All of them were attractive, except 18th Century.

1973-1988: ON THE JOB: Aside from French being a dominant interest, what sustained me during the years from 1963 to 1986 (minus 1973 to 1977) was my love for the humanities and the kinds of results one can actually see come alive through the books, music, art and human sweat and intelligence when involved in some facet of it. I became a member of the Mississippi Humanities Council and eventually became a board member. I learned all about the state of Mississippi, met Big Catfish in a small bowl, and talked with, and sometimes cajoled community leaders whose views were the exact opposite from mine (impossible to do at first, but I learned how to listen and nicely argue). I designed community programs, helped directors of projects, and offered different options to gaining solutions. We always had to travel to the location of the activity, which meant travelling with White, Black, Indian, Chinese, whoever was also on that sub-committee. Many an eyebrow was raised and many a frown was set when they saw all these di-ver-si-ties together. But that was part of our problem, to set up interracial programs with provocative contents, hoping that the people of Mississippi would begin to accept the inevitable. We made inroads, but not huge swathes of progress.

In tandem with the humanities was my rise in the foreign languages circles, first in- then out-of-state. I broke all kinds of records. During the 1960s-1970s, Mississippi had six White state-funded universities: Univ. of Miss., the flagship; Miss. State, the land grant university; and Univ. of Southern Miss., the free-floating university (big and multi-racial); Miss. University for Women, and two state-funded smaller ones, Delta State and Blue Mountain. There were three Black HBCUs: Jackson State University being the Black "flagship;" Alcorn State University, land grant; Miss. Valley State Univ.; and two private religion-based colleges: Tougaloo College and Rust College. Before the 1980s, all three dominant White universities, Ole Miss, Miss State, and USM, had a language major with education courses, and the M.Ed. degree for a Master's degree. All other universities offered two years or less, but their graduates could get jobs with just the two years offered by their schools. (Guess what kind of teachers graduated with permission to teach foreign languages!) And they did this with no thought to the graduates from the three Black schools who could teach better but could not get the jobs. I found myself in the role of rule-breaker. My being a "pedigreed" Black woman unafraid to be vocal helped me to talk back to anyone of any race on any level. I was also the only woman in the state of Mississippi who had a doctorate in such an "exotic" subject as French and from such a well-respected university as Florida State!!!

There was a strong State Foreign Languages Association, made up of all levels of language teachers and/or interested people, in academia or not. According to Mississippi standards, our association was the most "liberal" of all. We had to be, because what we taught was diversity itself, and how we taught was through communicating with each other. Every year a university would sponsor a statewide Foreign Language Fair, pitting the schools and individuals against each other in varied topical contests. And then we would have a once-a-year statewide meeting. We genuinely liked each other as people and professionals, and were glad for those two times a year to come together. I quickly found my niche in redesigning the fair, making more modernized contests, making friends for the languages, creating appropriate new prizes, from trophies on down to pins and ribbons and involving more teachers in very impartial judging processes. The university campuses volunteered or were asked to host the fair, which attracted over 800 students at its peak. I involved the university hosts by proving to them that the fair was an excellent recruitment opportunity; Food Services had a special noon meal for a low price, many departments offered tours and the Music Department used the time for auditions. In other words, it was a win-win situation for the universities when it rotated to them—it was a wonderful way to show off the college.

My partner Sarah and I (she was a professor of Spanish with a degree from Southern Cal. who moved to Jackson with her husband when he got a good job here) did a similar changeover to the Association of Foreign Language Teachers. We changed the format, altered the content, and made it respond to the needs of the FL teachers. My best contact was that I was on the board of the National SAT Board and my voice was loudest when I was fighting for Black high school students and teachers about the contents of this national test. I like to think that I changed the minds of many important White men and women, not so much to their faces but after and between meetings. Those national board members had as much clout as individuals, and I was able to give information to my Mississippi colleagues straight from the horse's mouth.

1976 – 1988: BACK ON THE JOB: I returned home from FSU with a Doctorate in Afro-French Literature in 1976. I had convinced Dr. Carrabino that he would find committee members because of the new spin on French literature, so he scoured the Humanities division for people he thought would be interested and found so many that he had to fight for spaces for our own Graduate French Department. Afro-French (or French-African, or Francophone, or Negritude) Literature was my topic and they were interchangeable. French-African Literature was totally new to some, and others did not understand the full range of it. It was the study of the literature from any French-speaking country. It explored the poetry, novels, cinema, philosophy, and history of French-speaking Africa, Haiti, Martinique and the smaller French-speaking islands of the South Pacific. Most of the literature came from Francophones (the result of mixed marriages) or Black artists of France, Africa, the Caribbean Islands, and Haiti. This period of literature coincided with or was made possible because of decades of colonialism. To study the literature meant also studying the philosophy, religion, art, music, history, and even the cinema of that country. My job was to expose this new literature to students (and many times, professors). It excited me then.... It is still fascinating to me now!

1976 – 1988: MY OTHER JOBS: I was appointed as chair of the JSU Department of Foreign Languages. My partner (Dr. Sarah J. Banks) and I immediately began laying the foundation to expand our curricular offerings to include a Bachelor of Science degree in French Education, Spanish Education and German Education. Our faculty was not strong enough yet to offer a comprehensive French Literature degree, and I knew it. But we had to start somewhere. These were exhilarating days, fighting to become (at least) The Black University to offer a major and minor in different facets of foreign languages. And the numbers began to change: Most good high schools in the state had White students with Black foreign language teachers who already had degrees from the three HBCU schools (but JSU was the main "feeder" and college instructors were already becoming aware of a difference in the students coming from them). It was all numbers and politics.

We were playing their game with no politics and less money. Ole Miss staff was under discreet orders to shut us down. When they made the move to ask the University Board to allow all foreign languages to be offered by only the Three Big Ones, the real goal was to stop ambitious JSU from expanding Liberal Arts courses. We had about three weeks to organize. Our plan was simple: Call out the Foreign Language cavalry and bring attention to the plan and offer an alternate plan. On the morning of the board meeting, Foreign Language aficionados from everywhere marched to where the board was meeting and somehow got some media time to explain ourselves. We marched and stood silently until our friends from Ole Miss stepped up to speak against the board permitting an aye vote. Temporary checkmate! It worked for the near future while both sides considered their next options. We lost, but the statewide community saw the White board in action and heard more blowing off air and thus began to debate and talk about Ole Miss's overall plan to take over Jackson State completely. We lost! We gained! The board voted down our request to add to the current curriculum (loss) and allowed us to keep what we had (a solid Bachelor's in Education for each foreign language (gain)). About twenty or so years later, our university president wrote his "Memoirs" and that was when I found out that he had made some sort of deal with the board not to fire me. I never knew....

I was still a department chair, but of what? And I was still a voting member of the all-powerful Curriculum Committee, which allowed me to keep up with how other departments were battling the board's temporary halt to their aggressive plans. No matter, we decided to go for gold with what we had, which was to strengthen the courses we had and to design some courses out of the line of fire. We became famous for developing different courses to satisfy the free option English hours (3) decreed by the Curriculum Committee. Good choice! We were in the game again, this time lower than before, but playing with their rules on our own playing field. The Humanities were still a large part of my life. I traveled, lectured, solidified friendships, met more Mississippians, and updated my opinions of the status of higher education here. Life was good—from that point of view! Another point of view was seeing what we had scratched and fought to build up during the sixties and seventies deteriorating, being destroyed, or disappearing from one state board meeting to the next, and wondering what our next move should be, aside from having multiple stress episodes and heart attacks.

All this time (up to the mid-eighties) I was still an active graduate advisor to the AKA Chapter, Gamma Rho. The ladies were strong-willed and convinced they could outtalk and overrule current important regulations and sorority leaders. I had had enough; I wasn't being rewarded in any way; I didn't need this. I had given all these years of my youth being sisterly and this is how I was treated. I tendered my resignation as graduate advisor and did all the paperwork needed to make a peaceful transition, at least with my regional director. Looking back on that period, I must admit that I was just tired. And the ladies were not what Alpha Kappa Alpha stands for. They were acting like spoiled brats who had lost their favorite toy, which is probably an apt description, since the AKA Directorate was thinking of how to stop hazing practices among members.

(Real self-talk:) Until! Another shocker—my husband Billy decided he wasn't satisfied with his job status at JSU and put out feelers for a job. And he got his dream job! At his alma mater, Morehouse College in Atlanta, as the registrar. (Secretly, he had always wanted to return to Atlanta and Morehouse. The problem was that his picture of Atlanta had become idealized.) Real problem: Our son would be in his senior year at St. Joseph Catholic High School, and he needed a father-figure. It would also be my 25th year at JSU, which meant I would be eligible for retirement. Billy K. did not want to change schools his senior year, so the decision was made that Billy Sr. would leave us and go to Atlanta to find housing for the rest of us. Billy K. would enroll at Morehouse College in the fall of 1989 and live with us in Atlanta. Mitzi had her Juris Doctorate with firm roots in Jackson and wanted to stay in our house. In a nutshell, the final decision was that I would remain in Jackson with Billy K. until June of 1989, and thereafter I would be eligible to work elsewhere without losing my pension.

1989 – 1999: Billy K. finished his senior year and I wound down my tenure at JSU. I was given a retirement party from JSU and made ready to relocate to Atlanta. Oh, and I had a job – as Associate Professor of French at Spelman College, Mitzi's Alma Mater.

I stayed at Spelman until 1993. It was sort of a dream job, what with Spelman's reputation and all. I was tapped to help with the Freshman Year Experience Program also (that's one thing about HBCUs, they use every bit of your physical and mental abilities), and later with Spelman's renowned

Study Abroad Program, which paid my way to accompany a group of students on a summer trip to Germany.

My position changed again. One of my required committees was my assignment to the UNCF-Mellon Program. I mentored students who vied for fellowship funds and experience working at selected colleges and universities while still undergraduates, with the proviso that they would find a job in Higher Education. I traveled a lot to conferences with the Fellows (called the Mellon Fellows) and generally kept tabs on their required research. The program was year 'round, what with all the choices they had. My boss was the Director of the Mellon Programs wherever such programs were offered. The goal for the Fellows was to do research on their chosen subject, do a presentation at the national meeting, and be paid doing it. Also at Spelman, I was tapped to be the Assistant Director of Freshman Studies and Associate Professor of French. The Mellon director was also my boss for this position. That new position made me responsible for keeping up with the individual student attendance at Wednesday (or was it Tuesday?) Chapel events, required at most HBCUs at that time, and a hot source of contention since most of the ladies would not go willingly. The Spelman students were exceptionally bright, but not necessarily malleable, as I found out, for instance, when a Spelman Sister exceeded the required number of absences from Chapel, she would pull out all stops not to have her grade affected.

Then came The Letter that changed everything. From the Mississippi Retirement Office: They could not find evidence that I had paid into the retirement system for four years, which meant I was drawing a paycheck illegally now. My pension would be cut off this year unless I found proof of paying, or got a job funded by the State System. (The irony of it all was that the MS State money sent to FSU for my tuition never came through me. The State sent the funds to JSU, who would send it to wherever for whomever.)

Three JSU colleagues were going to FSU during the same time. I made an emergency trip to Jackson to talk to the Powers-That-Be about the situation. No one knew anything, except that there had been a fire in the location where they kept those records, and my information could have been there. Oh, boy, I had gotten used to that second check! Returned to Atlanta with fallen feathers! And a burst bubble! It turns out though that people in Mississippi had been busy. I had bad-mouthed JSU legitimately about my retirement situation and someone had picked up on it. Before two weeks had passed, my Foreign Language friends at the University of Southern Mississippi called to tell me that they were negotiating terms for a job for me at USM with their president. All, even the president, were good friends of mine. I am told that the president (he had 20+ years of being president at this university) made one phone call to the right person, and voilà, before I knew it, I was talked into taking that job for the four years I was missing as Full Professor of French with a salary I thought I'd never get in this world, starting in September of 1993. I must rephrase a sentence I used earlier: "It was all numbers, politics, and money" (lol).

1993 – 1997: AT USM IN HATTIESBURG: I was kind of sorry to be leaving my good associates at Spelman and Morehouse, both of which had excellent foreign language programs. I had learned how to manage a unit with no budgetary crisis, and I had taken my first trip abroad. Atlanta reintroduced me to the world of cultural events, which had been fueled at Fisk, by the way. I would not miss negotiating Atlanta traffic jams or department store crowds or the real fast pace. Another memory which has resurfaced was the TV show *The Cosby Show*, which was hugely popular then. (I wonder what the sisters' reactions were to Cosby's guilty verdict of sexual abuse, and likewise to his most recent acquittal!) The center of the Spelman campus is a quadrangle surrounded by classroom buildings and dormitories and Sisters Chapel. No matter what the event was, such as when a very popular soap star on *The Guiding Light*, was written out of the show, windows opened, girls started crying and mourning, and in general, disturbed the usually quiet and somber academic atmosphere. The same thing happened with the Cosby episodes: The girls would loudly express their feelings in or out of the buildings and the sounds would reverberate around the campus. I liked that noise!

Here I am at Southern Miss/USM, and officially on the payroll. Finding an apartment was fairly easy because my Foreign Language friends had a list of "suitable" apartments in "suitable" environments. By the way, these are the same people who formed a group during our association days way back in the sixties, and then during our protesting days. I LOVE those guys, men and women. When I needed him, Billy would do long-distance approval by phone and camera pictures (that was all we had back then). This was the first time in my life living by myself and being totally responsible for everything. The four years seemed to fly by. This was my second time teaching White students en masse (back in Seattle with the rich middle school delinquents, remember?). USM was said to be quite "liberal," that is, for a university located in southern Mississippi! That "liberal" reputation must have come from the mostly out-of-state academics and students, because, close up and teaching them, the real personalities—racist with pro-slave mentalities, confronted me. But I was no crybaby or whiny person, or complainer. I usually could handle whatever the situation was.

This toughness evidently was noticed and it brought a "required" invitation to become a member of the University's Promotion and Tenure Committee. Remember, I was in a strange place, and I knew nothing about how a White university works, the standing rules, the dominant opinions, the internal politics, the perceived or real territories, etc. I asked the president why he had put me there, and he replied that my presence would keep them "legit"! Surprise, surprise! My teaching load was irregular, because of these other kinds of assignments. However, I did teach Intermediate French, Advanced French Grammar, two or three other graduate-level courses, and Freshman Orientation. But good things come to an end, and so would this.

But not before USM paid me extra to go to Montpelier in the south of France with a bunch of students for six weeks of school, made up of courses especially for American college students. I was immersed in French and self-made projects to spend my time usefully since the students were in class all day. I used the time well! The seventh week, we said au revoir to the beautiful coastal town of Montpelier and spent that last week in Paris doing the cultural tour thing. Billy had arranged to meet me there. Because of an embarrassing situation on one of the previous Study Abroad programs, each student had to write a letter to their parents or guardians detailing their plans for each day after they left me to go home or wherever. I would then make copies for USM and myself and I would personally mail them to their designated relatives. This is because earlier, some students disappeared after Montpelier and took an unexpected week's vacation without their families knowing where they were. That's why there was this mailing game. After they were gone, my husband and I had a good time during that week. I will always be thankful to the President of USM for making this time of my life a joyous one.

My third year, the president called me in and told me that he had given my salary a "generous" boost for these last two years, knowing that the system uses the last four years of employment to average out the beginning of the retirement salary. He had also looked with disbelief at my salary over the twenty-five years at JSU and reckoned that, under the circumstances, the President of JSU had done what he could for all his faculty with the funding he was given. He thanked me for the work I had done. USM gave me a retirement party (the third) that was a blast. Not the gift kind, but the good time kind. Faculty members that I did not even know came, seemingly sincere. My group was known for its food. After all, the foreign faculty used every event to show off their equivalent to our soul food. A good time was had by all. The next day I left USM to go home, to 5980! And immediately missed my apartment!

FALL 1997 – SPRING 1999: From Southern Miss to RUST COLLEGE, my next "assignment." Rust College is a small college in Holly Springs, MS, quite near to Ole Miss, with a close affiliation to the United Methodist Church system. I went with the title of Dean of Humanities, thinking there would be at least four departments under me. Not so: The Humanities Department was one tight-knit bunch of scholars who taught and administered their subjects, and left the money arguments with the Higher-Ups to me. There was one department (that was me) and various Humanities subjects gathered together on one floor of one building, except Music, which had to have a stage. The campus radio station was in my bailiwick too. I had never worked with a radio unit before, so I would be learning some new stuff. My disappointment was overcome by my curiosity: How did this kind of setup work? I was very curious about Rust because of its unique school calendar. Its school year ended in early April, there were three modules instead of two semesters and one month for a Christmas vacation, and the weekly teaching hours defied the normal college calendar. It took me a while to get used to it. Some faculty liked the calendar, others were totally against it.

I cannot say I did much of anything that would be a proud legacy to my being at Rust for two years. I think the most important thing was that I shook up the faculty's complacency and rattled their creative genes on how to impart their subject to their students in different ways. I would not accept mediocrity, no matter how it was delivered. They were good people, used to leaning the same way a strong wind blows. Until … they reclaimed their integrity and zest while watching their academic energy and interests return. This time my contract was not renewed for the third year. Again, that retirement party—the fourth! Afterthought: I really do believe some of the very personal remarks I received via notes and cards. The faculty was actually beginning to come alive the last three months of my tenure there. Therein lies the reward for teachers of any age and level. I feel good about the friends I made there, the students I touched, the curricular revisions (small stuff only) I led them through. And over time, tidbits here and there have informed me that my talks and requests still live.

FALL 2000 – SPRING 2010: AT TOUGALOO COLLEGE IN JACKSON

My former Dean of Liberal Arts at JSU invited me to revise a handbook to be used by freshmen at Tougaloo College in Jackson, Mississippi. That simple request led to a ten-year job with the Freshman Studies Program as a springboard. I was right at home (LOL) because quite a few former JSU faculty and administrators held off their final retirement by teaching at Tougaloo, and literally at home because my house was 1½ miles from the campus. Within that ten-year period, the administration moved me where they needed me, including Assistant Director of Freshman Studies and Dean of Liberal Studies. As was my style, I tried to stop fires as I perceived them coming instead of waiting for them to develop into full-fledged fires. I became known as the Faculty's Friend because I tried to protect them in various settings by asking the forbidden questions that the younger faculty was too insecure to ask. Also, my creativity in developing new courses was fully utilized. Three of the courses had been tried out at Jackson State in the eighties and the students weren't in the mood for trying new courses. At Tougaloo, their minds were receptive and they welcomed new approaches to the same-old-same-old academic challenges.

The Powers-That-Be asked the Liberal Arts Division Chair and me to mentor and work with a male senior who wanted to apply for the Truman Scholarship. Tougaloo had never won a Truman Fellowship but they, and we, had faith that this young man, Jarvis, had an excellent chance to claim it. This challenge stretched all my Humanities training, but it could have been much worse. Dr. Jackson and I brought together a team of intelligent and dedicated Jacksonians, Black and White, campus and non—we knew where the geniuses were hidden. My colleague and I worked up a study calendar for the entire year—Jarvis had indicated his desire way ahead of time. This young man had all the qualifications needed, including knowing his weaknesses and working harder on them, and a strong extended family support system. Really, all we had to do was check to see if he was keeping up with his classes and making him take time to relax. He was also a contender for valedictorian (he had all A's). To make a long story short, he blew away the interview process, and won the Truman. And was co-valedictorian—the other co-valedictorian was his best friend, and they both were English Literature majors. Oh, my, doesn't it take a community??!!!

For some reason, I could always rebuild different ways of doing what was requested. For example, I thought of a new way to improve English vocabulary, so that, given a chance, my students could use "proper" English in the right circumstances. The course was called English Word Power and I am told that Tougaloo students and faculty called for that course long after I was gone. It was not an easy course to teach because the instructor had to have some Latin, Greek, Anglo-Saxon, French, and German, plus a sense of humor to understand better the English of today.

One more example: I taught concepts of English Literature through reading iconic novels and other kinds of literature, some three and four centuries old. The course was called "The Law in Literature" and I used Golding's *Lord of the Flies*, Machiavelli's *The Prince*, Sophocles' *Antigone*, King's *Letter from a Birmingham Jail*, Shakespeare's *Hamlet*, Hugo's *Les Misérables*, Movie *High Noon*, and Sartre's and Camus' perspectives of Existentialism. I was in literary heaven teaching courses like this. And when a student from Spelman College wrote in her evaluation: "I feel ready to tackle graduate school now, because I just took my first graduate course."—Of such are personal successes measured.

In courses like this I often hark back to my Fisk, Atlanta University, and FSU training. Though years apart, my mind must have retained the way my instructors organized their contents. Their ability to jump around creatively brought about combinations that were not thought of before. And then the way they got students to regurgitate the contents so that the exams or papers could take off on their own flights of fancy was their reward, and mine too!

UP TO THE PRESENT: As I thought more and more about a final retirement, about saying a last hurrah, about being divorced from the collegiate atmosphere, I was so glad my last group of students came from Tougaloo College. I was happy that they got the best of my maturity with lectures and openly shared their thoughts and dreams of the future. Many things in my life were coming to a "full circle," which indicated that they were steps to closure. I had indicated to my boss that I would probably retire in June of 2010, but I was hospitalized in April or May of 2010 for a two-week stay to find out what was wrong. The doctors never could say definitely, except that it could have involved a vascular flow disorder. I did not return to Tougaloo's classrooms. But of course, the faculty threw a retirement party in July which brought out my friends from across the state as well as the locals. My special group of students came to tell me "Au revoir." This fifth one had all the elements of the other four, but there was an underlying sadness that this would be the last. After all, I was 73 years old and had been teaching for 50 years, 45 of those in HBCUs. I think I was simply WORN OUT!

And I had no professional or personal bubble anymore, not at that time. The Golden Edge (the two years ahead of many others my age) that Fisk had offered to me in realizing whatever they saw in that test had paid off in terms of my life-strand. But God was not through with me yet! I came alive in my bubble again around 2014 when my daughter surprised us. Background: Mitzi had won a scholarship to Spelman College which saw her through the undergraduate years. She also had pledged Mu Pi Chapter of AKA at Spelman, thus becoming my legacy. She won some sort of scholarship to Tulane Law School in New Orleans, finished her studies, and passed the Mississippi Bar in record time. She is coming up on her 30th year as Assistant U.S. Attorney for the Southern District of

Mississippi. She is married to James Paige Jr., a U.S. Marshal and entrepreneur. Her life was exponentially expanded when she ran for and won the South Eastern Regional Director position in AKA in 2017 and again for a second term in 2019. She is the latest Shining Star of the Dease-Paige Clan. (I can't really say that, because her Daughter #1 is an up-and-coming trailblazer, and has begun to spread her wings already.)

Speaking of AKA, my mother was the first AKA in our family, having pledged in 1946, the graduate chapter Alpha Theta Omega in Raleigh, NC. I am my mother's legacy. Mitzi also chose AKA, thus becoming a double legacy; Amber and Kellyn are AKAs and double legacies also.

I am a grandma, "Gammy," to SEVEN GRANDGIRLS. Mitzi has three girls, all of whom are now AKAs, and Billy K. has four girls, from 16 years old down to 9 years old. Both Mitzi and Billy K. have twins; Mitzi's two youngest are 20-year-old identical twins, and Billy K.'s oldest two are the 16-year-old fraternal twins. So, as you think back over what you have read, think also of the time and effort it took to raise two children and to help raise seven grandgirls. Billy K. is married to Trinette F. Dease, a highly talented interior designer and art teacher in the Jacksonville Public School System.

Abbreviated Word-Pictures of My Seven Grandgirls

Mitzi's Three: Bria, a summa cum laude graduate of Spelman College, is in her 3rd year at Rutgers University in Brunswick, NJ, striving for a Ph.D. in English Literature with a specialty in African-American Women's Literature; her goal: to be the college president of a(n) HBCU. Bria also received one of four $25,000 scholarships from BEYONCE Yes! BEYONCE!!!) two or three years ago. Her latest was a summer fellowship from NEH as one of two digital analysts in the newest addition of NEH,

Digital Humanities, working virtually from Jackson. Amber's passion is dentistry, and Kellyn's is to be a registered nurse. Both of them have full scholarships and are in their 3rd year at Tennessee State University in Nashville. Last year, Kellyn was elected Miss Sophomore and Amber was appointed Secretary of the Sophomore Class and they both joined AKA. They say that this year will be one of introspection! Ha!

Billy K.'s Four: Kamryn and Kayla, 16-year-old twins, are in the 10th grade in the Jacksonville School System, in a special school for honors levels and humanities subjects. Though it's a little early to tell, Kamryn is showing a propensity for art and drawing. Kayla doesn't want to commit to anything yet, but she loves books and reading. Kara, the 14-year-old, is still fishing around for the right subject or combination. The "baby" of the family, 9-year-old Kinley, is all over the place, and her preferences and interests are apt to change every day of the week! One thing about her, she is always entertaining and has a knack for asking the right questions.

KUDOS to those of us who shook off senioritis to pull together these Herstories 65+ years later. It was a daunting task to do, calling for something different from a BIO or a curriculum vita, and KUDOS x 2 for The Three who kept at it and kept jogging us until our brains awoke and produced these results!

Lastly, I would like to take this opportunity to express my heartfelt thanks to the Ford Foundation of long ago for taking a chance on me all those years ago. If the Basic College Program still exists, please do keep it going, for we still need such a program to feed and fuel our young ones, our next generation. If it no longer exists, I'll bet statistics over the years will prove that the Basic College Program was a win-win.

MISSION ACOMPLISHED!

Barbara Then and Now

Barbara w/mother the year before Fisk | Barbara in doctoral gown

Top: Inclusive Family portraits;
Center: Barbara and Mr. Dease: the Page Family;
Bottom: Daughter, Mitzi, Barbara and husbands; grandgirls.

Jane Geraldine Fort

I can hardly believe how much of my life falls into what people so easily call "coincidences." I am experiencing the 21st century as just another series of years although it always had seemed otherworldly, like science-fiction. And who knew I would ever experience being on faculty in an educational institution when that was the last thing on earth I ever intended? As the child of educators who were themselves children of educators, I decided early on that I would make my living being something, anything, other than a teacher. So I majored in what seemed the appropriate thing for someone who was a listening ear to all my friends: Psychology. It felt natural and seemed to call me. However, I did not take the clinical path; after entering graduate school I reveled in the resurgence of my early inquisitiveness and took the research route to discover just why people do the things they do. So, here I am experiencing retirement from a career in the educational sector, bemused at the ways by which I have come to this place.

My experiences at Fisk University shaped much of my career as well as my personal life, for I was a member of the Fisk family long before I entered as a college student. Nashville Tennessee's Negro (as we were called then) residents enjoyed social and intellectual lives centered around the higher education institutions in the neighborhood: Fisk, Meharry Medical College, and Tennessee Agricultural & Industrial State College, now Tennessee State University. The institutions are located within ten or so blocks of each other; Fisk and Meharry are across the street from one another. Our social activities included the performances and lectures offered by campus resources or via special guest programs. We children grew up attending the various baccalaureate and commencement services as well as the sports games along with the adults.

I spent my childhood on the campus of each school in the neighborhood. First, I was at Fisk in its nursery school and later on campus again as a private piano student and participant in the youth summer drama programs. I was at A&I where my mother, a graduate, Geraldine Bennett Fort, was on faculty, not only participating in their children's drama activities, but also as a high school student sitting in on a typing class that proved an essential benefit in my later education and career. During summer breaks from college, I had my first job as a research assistant on a Pediatrics Department project at Meharry Medical College where many of the associates of my parents and later my father, William Henry Fort II, were employed.

Fisk's preschool only offered nursery school for children three and four years old; when my friends and I turned five, there was no kindergarten available for Negro children anywhere in town. I had the opportunity to stay in a school setting by accompanying my father to Ford Greene Elementary School where he was principal. I sat in on the first-grade class and asked my parents for a tablet and fat pencil so I could copy my letters like the other children. On the last day of school and promotion to the next class, I was the only student who was to remain in the first-grade classroom. Since I had completed all the work with the other children, but the teacher said there was no reason for me to sit through the first grade again. I officially registered in elementary school starting in the second grade at age six. Being a student in the school where my father was principal made my life more difficult rather than easier. He and I both worked extra hard to see that I was treated like the other students. For the most part, we made it although some students were too ready to accuse me of receiving favors since my parents and the teachers were pretty hard taskmasters, I had just as much as or even more work to do than the others and at higher standards of expectation.

The experiences my friends and I had at Ford Greene, and later at Washington Junior and Pearl Senior high schools, were special. We not only learned our academic work and were given mature intellectual challenges, but also learned much about our history as a people. We were trained to be the vanguard of the next phase of the movement toward integration and were steeped in Negro history. Special guests were brought to the schools for weekly assembly. I have a photo of Ralph Bunche speaking to students at Ford Greene; he and my father knew each other at Harvard University where Daddy earned a bachelor's degree after having earned one from Fisk. Our pageants included the lives and experiences of famous Negroes. I still remember portraying Mary Mahoney, first Negro nurse. Imagine my surprise and delight when decades later my Boston neighborhood health clinic was named for her.

Our childhood included what was considered appropriate for well-educated youngsters in the 1940s and '50s. We were members of the Scouts and played in the marching bands and concert orchestras of our schools; most of us took private piano lessons as well. We participated in the children's drama opportunities offered by Fisk and by A&I. Several of us were also members of a girls' club with international focus as a result of the associations with Fisk's racially integrated faculty. This gathering of young Negro and White teen girls facilitated our exposure to the history, art, food and activities of other cultures, countries and continents. It was in one of these sessions that I had my first taste of Chinese food, now one of my favorites. Nashville was a pleasant and easy city in which to grow and mature. Our communities were resource-filled and neighborhoods were intact, safe and supportive. But I also remember the unsettling time during the Second World War: rationing, air raids, blackouts and troop trains. Nashville is a large city within driving distance of Kentucky's Fort Campbell Army Base so soldiers became a familiar sight in the neighborhood when they visited the social club on our block.

When I began my college years, I entered Fisk as a young and timid adolescent of 15, barely out of pigtails and ribbons. I was one of three students from the Nashville public schools to enter the two-year-old college preparatory program at the institution: the Basic College Program for Early Admission funded by the Ford Foundation. Since it was a "school within a school" and since it had planned excellent opportunities to keep us safe and protected while being intellectually challenged, I suppose it seemed perfect to my parents. My father and his parents were Fiskites, so it was natural for me to consider the program. The first I remember about the BC Program was my father mentioning that there was this standardized test opportunity approaching and it would be a good experience to get acquainted with that sort of test since it was the wave of the future. Some friends of mine and I took the tests, later learning we had passed the entrance requirements for the Fisk BC program and were eligible to begin college the upcoming academic year. While my parents were discussing the pros and cons, my only opinion was that I would not want to leave high school if I stayed through my junior year. For me, it was now or never, and essentially my parents' choice. I had always been attracted to books and reading so one school environment over another would not make a great difference. I entered Fisk the fall of 1953.

As BC students, our lives on campus were mixed with the usual college activities, but we had a dean specifically for our program and a number of activities that were parallel to those of the regular students. We not only lived in an all first-year-BC dorm but also took our evening meals together in the house dining room, weekly, or even more often, joined by a member of the faculty or administration. Our experience was designed as a protected one, keeping in mind our age, our number, and the need for this to be a positive experience for us. Our drama group was all BC while we were mixed with students in other campus activities. We matriculated in our assigned academic schedule putting some of us in classes with regular freshman students dependent on our high school curriculum; others of us were enrolled in classes comprised predominantly of other BC students. We were the third cohort in the program, so associated with those who had entered before us for many BC activities. We girls lived in Dunn House, formerly a personal home that had not been renovated as a dorm, but had plenty of bedrooms in addition to the downstairs social areas.

Life on campus was quite enjoyable for me. I had "sisters" around all the time. I had grown up in a household of two children; my sister, Dorothy Kathryn, is several years younger, so our years together were spent playing with those closer to our ages rather than with each other. The BC fellows in my entering year were like brothers and we all studied and socialized as one large group. Most of us entered at age 15 or 16, so the close experiences youngsters usually have at those ages while in high school, we had with each other in the BC program; essentially we matured together. By second year, we were more integrated into the fabric of the institution, but still separate. Those of us who had come from the 10th grade continued to have an almost all-BC experience before we joined the college sophomore class, our graduating class, giving us a five-year college experience.

All through my years at Fisk, I was enrolled in classes taught by professors seasoned in their disciplines, many of them in retirement. Dr. Charles S. Johnson was the president during most of my years on campus and made a point of capitalizing on his many contacts in the world of social science; we were exposed to a wealth of ideas and perspectives throughout our time at Fisk. A major part of my socialization and integration into Fisk campus life was to pledge Alpha Kappa Alpha Sorority, Inc., during my third year. While the pledge experience brought me into closer intimacy with the sophomores who were now class and pledge peers, it also brought greater space into the close-knit original BC group, so broadened my friendship networks preparing me well for my exchange to California's Whittier College that spring semester. Five other students also were exchange students to California that year, three to Whittier and three to Pomona College, becoming the "Negro Presence" within those institutions. We took courses that met some of our requirements, but primarily explored and shared other perspectives and ways of being in the world. I repeated the pledge experience by joining one of the Whittier sororities.

Fisk prepared me admirably for my graduate school years. My generation was the one that broke color barriers everywhere as legal segregation began to end. We had been trained to be the best, even better than the best in order to have an opportunity at being admitted to higher education, at being hired, at being recognized and acknowledged for our work. It was made clear to us that we were not only a reflection on ourselves and on our families, neighborhoods and schools, but were representing the

Negro race at all times and in all of our activities. Of course, at the time, we could not know how thoroughly we were being prepared in the ways of the world in which we would spend the rest of our lives.

My first in-depth knowledge of the world of the Northern United States, including its weather, was in my graduate school years. Attending the University of Massachusetts in Amherst, I would have stood out even if I had not been the only Negro graduate student on campus: I was always taking pictures. I had never seen leaves so red or snow so deep. And I had never even heard of or seen a snow sculpture. I lived in a room in a home only a few short blocks from campus, so I made the campus, and especially my department, my homes for the two years I lived there.

I was sought out and befriended by a professor who had grown up in the Southern states and who became one of my doctoral advisors. We had interesting conversations sharing experiences from "down home." One year, he arranged a session in which I, and a local White student, talked about personal life experiences to help increase racial understanding and acceptance, or "tolerance" as it was called in those days. At the time, there was one Negro male in the undergraduate school and one Negro family living near town; we stopped and talked whenever we saw one another for we had no activities in common to bring us together.

Interestingly enough, I was the first of my ten-person class to complete my work. I entered the program as a Master's candidate in Psychology, planning to stay for the two-year program then begin educational counseling. Another of those "coincidences" was that my applications to grad schools had included this one last "why not?" application to U Mass. I applied primarily because I had experienced rewarding summers counseling at a camp in Massachusetts and especially enjoyed its piney woods. Of my various applications, this particular

Psychology Department offered me a full fellowship for my first year. I later learned that while all of the fellowship applications that year were comparable, I stood out as the only applicant with career-related experience gained administering Stanford-Binet tests to children during those summers I had spent on that research project in Pediatrics at Meharry. So, with the fortuitous "coincidence" of a fellowship, the die was cast and I enrolled. When the fellowship ended after that first year, I became research assistant in a faculty member's program on learning behavior in children from which I was later able to develop my individual projects for my Master's and Doctorate degrees.

My grad department was growing and expanding its goals. At the end of my second year when time came to take my Master's comprehensive exams and orals, collect my degree and move on, there was another "coincidence." The department faculty decided to emphasize the Doctorate and award Master's degrees after the requisite coursework and a thesis. Having already completed these, I essentially held the Master's degree that day with no further stress and strain, so I decided to stay on for the Doctorate, continuing the research assistant work I had begun. Although I had to complete some electives and doctoral comprehensive and language exams, I was well on my way to becoming the first "doctor" in the Fort family. I wrapped up my formal schooling in two more years, earning a Doctorate in Psychology and minor in Sociology coming out into the real world in 1962.

It was at a national job fair in New York City that I "happened" upon the job that began my professional career. I was offered a one-year research assistantship on a multicultural project housed at then Hunter College in New York. I remember looking over the job description and deciding that

I could deal with anything for a year, so I could consider this position. Although I had been looking for something, anywhere, I had specifically been looking for work that was NOT in NYC, feeling it was too big, too noisy, too dirty, too cold, too everything I had ever heard for me to work there. I took the job and found I not only enjoyed it but the city as well.

The decision to take the one-year job in New York was one of the best I ever made. This project put me in New York City in 1962 with colleagues also in Psychology, so I had a ready-made work and social group. Most of us kept in contact through the years with one relationship even continuing into retirement sharing information about life's issues: career options, marriages, children, divorces, aging parents, retirement. I have been very fortunate in making true and close friends from colleagues and coworkers through the years. However, I always remind myself and caution others not to attempt to make friends into coworkers; I have seen that transition backfire too often although the reverse seems to work quite well.

I still live off of the experiences I had those three years in NYC. It ruined me for some things; I don't get as excited about the entertainment that comes to town as much as I would otherwise, because, in so many instances, "I saw it on Broadway." I was a young professional in NYC and learned to enjoy all that the city had to offer by seeking out inexpensive and no-cost activities, a practice that served me well and allowed me to fully enjoy life in New York City. A special bonus was that I had a "homey" there. George Houston Bass had also grown up in Nashville and in those early years Nashville was segregated so just about everyone knew everyone else through school or church or the neighborhood. George also attended Fisk and he and I kept our contact and friendship through college and after; he had been in New York City for a few years having gone there to do his grad work in math. By the time I arrived, he not only knew the city and people and places, all of which made my entry to such a big and busy place easier and comfortable, but, as a result of having assisted Fisk's president's office in hosting guest dignitaries, had met and become assistant to Mr. Langston Hughes, subsequently turning his own career emphasis to literature and drama. Through George, I had opportunities to interact with Mr. Hughes, his extended family and their social network on a personal basis.

Much to my surprise, my one-year initial employment in New York zipped by far too quickly. I stayed in NYC employed on a grant that addressed the troubling times seen by inner-city youth in the Black and Spanish neighborhoods. Again, I met some lasting friends while trying to develop and implement programs to meet all the various needs—those of the youth, the city government, and the ethnic communities. I admit that my brief but active period in city-sponsored programs had quite an unexpected influence on me as I learned how decisions are not always made according to what is best for the most needy clients, but are limited by the restrictions of challenges faced in balancing competing interests of many other groups, a necessary albeit heart-wrenching lesson.

In another "coincidence," my boss from the first job, who in the mid-1960s moved to the Harvard University Graduate School of Education, contacted me about joining his staff. It was a special experience to be employed at the institution my father had attended. At HGSE, we replicated the project from NYC looking at the environmental and racial components of intellectual expression. It was most interesting to observe the similarities and differences among children of the same ethnic and social class groups as well as those across ethnicity and socioeconomic class. And now, decades later, the country is still challenged to address the disparities in class and racial opportunities and experiences.

I was at Harvard when increased attention was being paid to racial and ethnic equality. My national professional group, the Association of Black Psychologists, ABPsi, was formed in a caucus session at the California meetings of the American Psychological Association. Those of us there met and selected several topics that needed direct challenge. We left the meetings with the charge to form chapters in our local areas. On my return, I called together the first Black caucus of Harvard faculty and professional staff. It was not a difficult task since there were so few of us there then. In fact, I had been the second Black professional-level female employed in HGSE, a perfect set-up for that joke that was not a joke in those years. Upon first meeting me at a faculty social, a colleague said, "You must be So-and-So." I had to point out that I was "the other one" for there were now two of "us" there. By the time I left Harvard, four Black professionally trained females had been employed at HGSE. One has since passed, but I keep in touch with the other two. Nothing matches the experiences shared in those early days of integration. I spent nearly twenty years in the Cambridge/Boston area, the major portion of my early career and thirty/forty-something years. Cambridge was a refuge of sorts from the city that was New York in the mid-1960s.

My years in the Greater Boston area were filled with exciting and challenging experiences. Coming from a research background, I was particularly attuned to and interested in how best to protect the community from inappropriate and unscrupulous research efforts, one of the topics we had discussed in our ABPsi caucus meetings. When the agencies in Roxbury, Massachusetts, formed the Boston Black United Front after the assassination of Dr. Martin Luther King Jr., it was the perfect opportunity to form a sub-committee of the front. The resulting Community Research Review Committee was comprised of professionals who met regularly and reviewed research proposed for implementation in the community in an effort to identify any benefits that would accrue to its residents. Our efforts were modeled by others and continued for over a decade; major research institutions came to acknowledge the relevance of the issues, respect the community-focused perspective and establish their own research review boards.

I was also involved on a longitudinal public school childcare research project, the Brookline Early Education Project working with parents and children from birth through entry to kindergarten. BEEP sought to identify the programs and resources that would enable children to mature to their maximum during their preschool years. Being a part of a project that supported parents and their challenging task was particularly rewarding since by that time I was also a parent and so had personal knowledge of parenting issues.

I had met and married George Joseph Morrison while in Cambridge/Boston and had become a stepmother to his six-year-old son, Gregory Jonathan Morrison, as well as a homeowner. Our son, Sékou Fort Morrison, was born in Boston and spent his first ten years there in the midst of the Roxbury community development era. George, a community organizer, directed one of the local community development organizations, the Roxbury Action Program, so we were actively involved primarily in housing as well as other initiatives and fully supported the local community schools that had been founded to "turn the public schools around." While the neighborhood was changed in substantive, exciting, even dramatic ways, at ten years of age and by then the child of divorced parents, Sékou needed a change of venue and mostly more freedom than he could ever be given in Boston. An opportunity in Davis, California, appeared.

Not only was the move to California at a good time and to a good place for Sékou, it was also right for me. I "happened" into a job at the Early Childhood Education Center of the University of California at Davis in the early 1980s. I never expected to get back out to the West Coast for anything other than visiting after completing my semester as an exchange student to Whittier College. I had the opportunity to work at UCD for a couple of years just when we needed to vacate the Boston area for more and safer space and less stress. While I knew of and had utilized the various services and programs in our Roxbury neighborhood, I felt I was not able to allow Sékou the freedom of movement he wanted and needed at his age.

One of the specific reasons I sought employment in California was to be closer to family. My sister, Dorothy, called Dot, was working at IBM-Los Angeles and my widowed mother, Geraldine Bennett Fort, had by then married a childhood friend living in Hawaii, William J. Hale II, older son of William J. Hale, first president of Tennessee A&I College; his daughter and her family lived in Long Beach, California, where the Hales would gather. The idea of being closer to family was attractive. Sékou, Dot and I visited Hawaii and were smitten with the landscape, the people, the rhythm, everything. I started looking at what was available at institutions in California and the Pacific area and was even offered a job in Fiji, but had already accepted the one at UCD. We have been eternally imprinted by the sight of daily rainbows, and now keep crystals hanging in various windows to recreate as much of the experience as we can. I learned about the effects of folk medicine and alternative approaches to healing, along with the positive effects of living daily in a gorgeous physical environment.

Davis' smaller and more manageable university town environment allowed the freedom of movement as well as the mental space needed at the time. We joined the Black families in town who had formed a small, casual social group. Even so, Sékou was usually the only black child in most of his regular activities, disconcerting on one hand, but protective on the other. While we were frequently the only Blacks except when with the other families, there were hardly any overt instances of individual prejudice encountered by either of us, and everyone knew who Sékou was or at least how to get him to or in touch with someone who knew. I remember hating that fact when I was his age growing up in Nashville, but appreciating it as a parent, as I am sure my parents had.

Sékou and I were bicycle commuters in Davis, called by the locals, the "Bicycle Capital." It was great fun biking everywhere for everything, even in their winters that consisted mostly of rain of ten minutes or less. I rented a house, sight unseen, that "coincidentally" was:

1. For rent by an owner who had no experience; for example, she did not accept a security or month-in-advance deposit I offered because "you may not like it." That response let me know we were definitely in for a new experience;
2. At the end of a cul-de-sac;
3. One-story, with back and front yards that matched my southern upbringing and afforded our two cats a normal indoor-outdoor life;
4. Two blocks from the local supermarket;
5. Three blocks from the neighborhood elementary school;
6. Adjacent to the only park in town that I later learned offered an after-school program.

I was able to enroll Sékou in his new school for fifth grade and get him a house key; he bought a bicycle the first morning there. I learned about the park's program only after I also learned that I would be teaching a late afternoon course that dismissed at 6:00 P.M., the same time that the after-school program ended. For the years we were there Sékou came home only a few minutes before I arrived. Clearly, these were NOT "coincidences." This was Divine Order.

One of the most dramatic impressions California made on me was the abundant fruit trees growing everywhere; no one seemed concerned that the fruit was wasting in the yards and streets all over town. Coming from Boston with its six months of winter weather, it was all I could do not to gather the huge grapefruit orbs and ship them back East. Having sun and outdoor fun all year long was another dynamic experience. We had only rain for winter, and bright sunlight even on rainy days. As February approached just as I was hunkering down to make it through the last vestiges of winter, I learned that winter was over. Grass seemingly grew greener, trees blossomed, flowers bloomed. What an environment in which to spend one's days!

For the two years we were in Davis, the mechanics of daily living and raising a child were simplified and I also was reminded of what an excellent learning experience I had been given by my schooling in Nashville, especially at Fisk. I was dumbfounded one semester when one of my junior year students said I was the only teacher who had ever called her by name. Astounding to me because in my educational experience, we complained that all the teachers not only knew who we were but took occasion to speak to us about what and how we were doing in grade school and in college, whether or not we were enrolled in one of their classes. Growing up living within a segregated minority population within a majority-dominated environment, I saw that we really did live in a "different world" from the general culture of the country.

In Davis, Sékou was able to enroll in several enrichment classes: karate, cartooning. computer programming, German, gymnastics. I was able to experience a wealth of activities that reduced the pressure of being the sole person responsible for myself and for a minor child in a place where I knew absolutely no one else. The bicycle races I happened upon one weekend were a delight as was the Whole Earth Festival that came each year. The early-morning aroma of tomatoes being prepared at the Campbell Foods canning factory was a pleasant surprise along with the skydiving tournament. We were introduced to hacky sack, developed a new appreciation for Frisbee and for dog races that in Davis are run by the individual household pets of residents rather than by professional canines. We experienced the variety of religious services in town and often took the thirty-minute ride to Sacramento, sometimes attending Unity Church services there and also affiliated with the congregation some miles out of Davis that was led by a Native American woman who, along with her Baptist minister co-pastor, shared her culture's perspective on life. We spent a day in Yosemite National Park, visited the mummies in the Northern California museum and got down to the San Francisco coast for entertainment and seafood.

The West Coast/Pacific Ocean experience was a defining one for me. It was so refreshing to move from Boston where there were still efforts to ban books, to live where all people and ideas were welcomed. In California, it appeared that no one and nothing would be considered sufficiently different to be cause for condemnation. I came back East with an attitude of increased acceptance and the confidence that Sékou would forever be open to all peoples and styles and cultures, secure enough to select what was meaningful for him and for his life.

When my position at UCD was restructured out of existence and I was unable to locate other employment in California, Hawaii or various Pacific islands, I returned East. Sékou, Dot and I rode Interstate 40 from California to Nashville, seeing the Grand Canyon and Painted Desert and most especially watching the topographical map come to life as we left dry desert areas and entered green Southeastern states. Sékou and I stayed a year in Nashville; it was my first time living in my hometown as an adult. I began to see that, yes, you can go home again; the imprint was made for my more permanent return in the late 1990s. After a year in Nashville where I finally realized I had returned to a city that was desegregated but not integrated, Sékou and I moved to Atlanta which proved an enjoyable and rewarding experience.

The Atlanta University Center cannot be bested for broad exposure to African-American ideas and activities; our in-depth experiences in three of its seven institutions was exciting. I was relieved, though, to escape just before having to face Atlanta's hosting of the 1996 Olympics. The Black presence in Atlanta was welcoming. Particularly in Davis, and sometimes even in Nashville, Sékou and I had been "the only" far too many times. When we arrived, I was able to tell him he would finally meet people who would be familiar with his name and for whom he would no longer need to repeatedly pronounce or spell it. The city's biennial arts celebration, the National Black Arts Festival, was soul-satisfying each time I attended. Atlanta was also where I would learn how to relate to my son as an adult. We spent his middle and senior high school years in Atlanta and continued to visit one another after I left and he remained there attending Morehouse College.

Atlanta is where my career took me into the healthcare arena. Before being employed in a faculty support position in the Morehouse School of

Medicine Department of Community Health and Preventive Medicine, I first assisted faculty at then Clark College, now Clark Atlanta University. It was rewarding to work with faculty through Clark's Center for Faculty Development supporting efforts to access resources and to enhance faculty growth in completing more advanced degrees and publications. At MSM, among similar and other duties, I coordinated the Atlanta/MSM version of a joint consortium grant housed at Nashville's Meharry Medical College to ascertain health promotion and disease prevention information and status from the local Black communities. The project offered the chance to discover attitudes and perceptions of African-American adults in the Southeast regarding their risks for cancers and their behaviors to reduce those risks. Of course, identifying those perspectives involved many activities and interactions that were also excellent learning fields for individual and institutional behaviors.

I returned to Nashville from Atlanta to be my mother's full-time caregiver in what became her final illness. The experience forced me to bring up and utilize all I had learned after my father's death. I also finally understood about letting someone go. I could hear and see that my mother was ready to take the next step in this Eternal Journey we call life; "giving her permission" was probably the hardest thing I have ever done. My father's death decades earlier was a sudden blow to us all. He had had successful open-heart surgery and been released from care to return to his regular activities. He died of a heart attack the morning before he was to return to work. I was actually packing to spend time with him while my mother tended to some healthcare needs of her own when she called to say he had died.

Daddy's death put me back into earlier readings on death and dying. Of course, reading for classes and professional work and reading for personal comfort and understanding are different. I began to look for information to help me cope with this new experience of parental death and found much informative material. Near-death experiences had gained popularity in research and writing since Daddy's death and Mamma had also described Daddy's recounting of seeing light and experiences from his past flash before him during his physical trauma. We did not know then that what he described was typical, studied, and named. It opened me to readings that have influenced my perspective and led me to a broader exploration of scientific, philosophic and religious ideas, including those from other cultures. I continue exploration of religion and spirituality, finding an attraction in Eastern philosophies. I first encountered yoga in my thirties in Boston and practiced it for decades as a regular activity, even after leaving but found it a challenge when I came to Nashville. It was considered odd in the Southeast but has grown in acceptance and popularity in this new century.

I had taken leave from work to be my mother's caregiver; after her death, I gradually moved back into the professional world, reaffiliating with the cancer prevention project by joining its base at Meharry, the institution where I first began employment while in college, employment that ultimately shaped my career. I liked the symmetry of it all and I continued my interests and activities in the educational arena; it still "fit" even though I had originally attempted to avoid it as a career option. It was personally rewarding to maintain and further my interest and activity in ways to create healthier communities. I also coordinated a pre-medical program helping aspiring healthcare professionals master the skills required for such a career. I increased my contact with Fisk, serving in various volunteer and paid capacities on the campus. I especially enjoyed the opportunity to teach my favorite course, Human Development, in the department from which I was graduated and I was particularly supportive of the campus art galleries and the alumni association, even returning to the campus in its program for visiting alumni.

I learned while "out in the world" that I could be an "artist" without being able to draw a straight line, and after grad school took up pottery for nearly a decade. I dabbled a bit in fabric design while in Davis and became active and continued in retirement as a member in the local Gaiete de Coeur Art and Study Club, a Black women's club that has been in continuous existence in Nashville for nearly 100 years.

I have enjoyed the various stages of my life with its peaks and valleys. "Happening" into employment in educational settings has afforded me an interesting and rewarding work life. I have been employed and lived in five states in four regions of the country, so I have had a chance to experience various regional personalities, each, of course, so different from each of the others. I am still finding fascination in why people do what they do. That captures my attention no matter what the context, even what my own choices mean. Throughout my career experiences, beginning in graduate school, I was interested in and able to write and publish articles about the various projects in which I had been engaged, still attempting to learn and describe the why of human behavior.

I am back in my family's home "clearing out," which is a task I have performed—no, not past tense—have been performing since my mother died decades ago. As a most conscientious and focused organizer, I don't know how I have not completed and moved on from this task to other things. Am I stuck in this process? Psychologists say that if you do not complete life's experiences at the usual and expected time while in one of its many stages of growth and development, you will find yourself immersed in those issues at some later time. So, I suppose my life now is the late manifestation of what otherwise could have been a midlife crisis. But, if so, it doesn't feel like I thought "crisis" would feel. And so, I continue more or less at ease in my circumstances albeit eager underneath it all to get on with the business of living the experiences now available to me in this 21st century.

Jane Then and Now

Ellena Auxvasse Stone Huckaby

I was born in Houston, Texas, to parents French F. Stone, a prominent businessman, and Anne Elizabeth McIntosh Stone, both of whom were Fisk graduates. My roots can be traced backward through several generations in Texas and New Orleans, Louisiana, and there are other connections which came from West Africa, the Dominican Republic and southwestern Europe.

Attending public schools in Houston, I found myself in high school, facing an undecided future without a definite plan. My sister, Rosemary, had already enrolled in college at Fisk University, and was now a sophomore. When I was in the tenth grade, I went to visit her and learned that the Ford Foundation was seeking students for its Early Entrant Program. I'd had so much fun that weekend, I decided to follow my mother's suggestion to take the IQ and admissions tests for the program which had begun the year before. Although I was petrified at the thought of taking my first standardized test, my mother encouraged me to take action while I was already there on the visit. I braved the test, passed it with flying colors and was accepted into the Early Entrant Program designed for Black students with a high IQ. So in the fall of 1953, I was on my way to Fisk University!

The train slowly rolled to a stop, and finally suddenly lurched forward. Blowing a giant snort of steam, it finally came to a halt. Rosemary and I quickly gathered our luggage and grasping the porter's hand, stepped down onto the train's steep steps and high iron stool before touching the endless concrete platform of Nashville's train station.

The conductors pointed us "that-a-way" toward the giant clock tower, and we walked behind a giant wooden rolling cart with luggage cascading and sometimes falling over the sides. As we neared the giant clock, there stood the Fisk boys identifying themselves as Fisk students by an occasional Fisk cap or cardigan sweater, explaining that they would drop our luggage off at our dormitories if we would sign a ledger and pay the required fee. Since we were unable to use regular taxis, they motioned us toward a special group of taxis reserved for Black people only.

I already felt lonely as soon as Rosemary told the driver to drop me off at Dunn House first while she stayed "put" for her continued ride to the Scribner Hall dormitory. Dunn House was a forlorn-looking grey two-story house with a grey uncovered porch; this would be my home along with the other Early Entrants for our entire first year. Through the dark screen door of the house, I heard girls' voices; thereafter, a friendly, motherly-looking, fair-skinned woman named Mother Holtz swung the door open for me and my one large suitcase. (I would wait for my other bags and foot locker to be delivered much later.) I missed Rosemary even more and wished that she could visit to help get me settled, or better yet: Mama!)

I followed Mother Holtz up the stairs and into a dimly lit bedroom with bunkbeds. I chose the top one. Thereafter, I followed her downstairs to the dining room where dinner was being served. Seated at a long table, the other girls were settled in, having arrived days earlier either with their mothers or alone. (I was late because I had to wait for my sister who was a junior that year and could travel at a later time.) All the girls were quiet, shy and whispered a lot. I joined them while Mother Holtz claimed her place at the head.

The days to follow offered exciting views of the campus: many sites of interest, but particularly the Art Gallery. Fisk reinforced my love of the arts and all of its facets—dance, literature, visual arts, etc.; it was like the Harlem Renaissance for me. We studied art history under the famous visual artist Aaron Douglas, library science under Arna Bontemps, along with other academics such as mathematics, literature and foreign languages. August Meier was our Professor for History of Western Civilization. I found him to be eccentric and rather odd. (I didn't know at that time that he was the author of several books, and that he had taught in other HBCUs and that he was an activist in civil rights.). Herr Ferdinand Gowa, a refugee from Germany, was my German teacher (I was the only girl in my class with the boys headed to med school). "Fraulein Stein!" he would yell, give them the answer—he would say to me in German.

While at Fisk, I excelled in Spanish, French and German, and eventually majored in Foreign Languages. I would go on to teach first-year Spanish on closed circuit television to Fisk freshman. I became an Exchange Student at Pomona College in Claremont, CA, where I was the only student of color. One of my finest hours was spent initiating the successful desegregation of the Claremont, CA, Public Library. I protested to the Pomona College president and my professor my inability to obtain a library card after three attempts to check out a copy of *Little Black Sambo* for a paper I was writing about the profound impact negative images of Black characters had on young Black children. The president made sure I received a library card and I made an A+ on that paper! My only other A+ of which I am proud was earned in Astronomy class, taught by brilliant professor August Meier primarily conducted on the roof of the Academic Building. We had large telescopes and measured the distances between stars on some of the coldest nights of the year. Again, I was the only woman in the class.

My social life was full: I enjoyed membership in the AKA sorority and became a Kappa sweetheart at Fisk and Meharry. We attended various sports events, attended concerts in the chapel (of those given by music students as well as by renowned artists during Fine Arts Week). Although there were plenty attractive men to date, I did not seriously set my sights on anyone until after completing my work.

I graduated Fisk University cum laude in 1958, with a Bachelor's degree in Foreign Languages, and also earned my Master's degree from Fisk in 1960. Sometime later, I attended Rice University for additional studies in Art History, Contemporary Art and African Art—a decision which would prepare me for a second career in art gallery work and interior design.

I began my career as an educator and taught Spanish at Fisk, my alma mater. In 1962, I moved to New York with my husband, where I was selected by the Kennedy administration as chairman of the Language Arts Pre-Employment Program, and taught and mentored college and high school dropouts not only in reading and writing, but also in developing life skills necessary for successful employment. Working with young adults in Harlem was the beginning of my devotion to the development and advancement of the Black community.

Moving back to Houston in 1968, I worked as a teacher and personnel director hiring principals, teachers and supporting staff. While taking time off from full-time employment to raise a family, I remained involved in the community through volunteer service at Shape Community Center, St. James Episcopal Church, became a docent at the Museum of Fine Arts and cofounder of the Black Arts Center in Fifth Ward, Houston, Texas (the first Black art gallery, theatre and community arts center there).

In 1986, I returned to the world of full-time employment and expanded on my commitment to community development through the arts, working at the New York City Commission on Daycare in New York City, in Public Affairs and Events Planning under the office of Mayor Koch. Moving back to Houston in 1987, I took a position as Director of Placement and Alumni Affairs at Texas Southern University's Thurgood Marshall School of Law, developing internship and professional placement opportunities, seminars and personal coaching for law students and alumni. Starting in 1990, I worked in the Houston Independent School District in various capacities for over 15 years, developing the character education program: Best Friends, an empowerment and success-oriented program for 500 girls focusing on character building, personal life skills, decision making, physical fitness, pre-employment and college prep. Later, I worked with the office of the mayor to coordinate the SPARK Park Program which created parks in HISD schools with a public art component. Working with landscape architects and local artists, the execution of this won a White House award.

After retiring from employment at HISD and TSU, I became an entrepreneur, starting my own art dealership, Fine Arts of the African Diaspora. By chance, after visiting my home and admiring the interior, a collector asked me for the name of my interior decorator. When I indicated that I was the decorator, the collector hired me to do her home in NYC, and with that job, my interior design career began.

Moving back to New York on a part-time basis, I began the interior design business with clients including The Abyssinian Baptist Church for whom I designed and decorated offices of: the Development Corporation, the Reverend Dr. Calvin Butts, the ministerial staff, the bookstore and various private residences and spaces for commercial clients in New York, Houston and Los Angeles. My community interior design projects include the Ennis Francis Apartment Building in NYC, The Naturally Occurring Retirement Community, a nonprofit organization in NYC and the Odell Clark Condominiums in NYC.

I commissioned portraits and original artwork and created special collections for the Abyssinian Church including Ceremonial Ethiopian Art and Coptic Crosses, African-American Quilts for the Naturally Occurring Retirement Community, the James Vanderzee photograph collection, and other developed art collections.

My honors have included: Foundation Scholar and Blue Ribbon Scholar; special appointments on three separate occasions to the Texas Committee for the Humanities by the Governor of Texas; Vice Commissioner for two terms of the Houston Municipal Arts Commission; member of the Special Task Force for Houston Arts. Along with friends and colleagues in Houston, I am a founding board member of the Houston Museum of African-American Culture; have served as trustee for 15 years at the Museum of Fine Arts, as well as a member of the Education Committee and the Glassell School Committee. I also cofounded the African-American Art Advisory Association at the Museum of Fine Arts Houston as well. My public service continued as a board member in charge of community outreach at Houston Ballet and on the special events committee of the Houston Grand Opera. I have also been a board member of the Blaeffer Gallery at the University of Houston and a board member at MECA (Multi-Ethnic Cultural Arts) where I developed programming for Hispanic and African-American artists for Houston public schools; of the Ebony Opera Guild; The Ensemble; the Society for the Performing Arts and was a consultant and docent of the Menil foundation and the Rice University Museum.

Today, I am an art dealer and interior designer and the owner of Fine Arts of the African Diaspora, an art dealership and virtual gallery concentrating on contemporary art and antiquities created by people of African descent. I am also a member of The Links and the Girlfriends and am the proud mother of three children: Joi Collette Huckaby Rideout, Eric Stone Huckaby and Mevyn Everett Huckaby II; and quite the active hands-on grandmother of six grandchildren: Max, Kendall, Beny, Nicole, Matthew and Francois.

I am still friends with my classmates from Fisk and treasure my days there, then and now.

Ellena Then and Now

Ellena, daughter Joi, father and other Family Members

Other Photos:

Top: Reunion at Donna's Home. L to R: Jackie W., 4th Carol P., Jane Fort. 6th, Maryann, Barbara C., Donna, Jeanne 11th, Hildred @ piano.

Middle from L: Niara Sudarkasa (Gloria), Donna, Jacqueline Walton Sadler, Hildred

Bottom from L: Donna, Jacqueline McNeill James, Jacqueline W. Sadler , Maryann

Basic College

36 *The FISK News*

Basic College. Front Row, L to R: Jane, 4th; Maryann, 5th; Ellena, 6th; Second Row:, Hildred, 3rd; Donna, 5th. **Dunn House Girls,** Top Row: Donna, ; Ellena, Jackie Walton, Carol Pindle; Second Row: Jeanne, 2nd; , Gloria; Front Row, Barbara C., D. Crippens; Jane, Maryann, Hildred

Dunn House Girls: Donna, Ellena, Jackie W., Carol, top; Jackie M, Jeanne, Barbara, Donnette, Jane, Maryann and Hildred, front

AKAs: Front Row:. L to R: Barbara, 3rd, Ellena, 5th; Jane. 7th; Donna. 11th;
Back Row: Hildred. 3rd, Maryann, 5th, Crippens, 9th, Jacquelyn M., 10th

reading from left to right: (front row) ann dickerson, margaret mills, barbara crockett, douglas bowe, dr. gladys forde, dr. lillian voorhees. (second row) joan morrow, elestine simmons, charles gerald, norma mc claffie, margaret james, john harper. (third row) john parker, robert sedus, carolyn birchett, delores rendleman, larkin landers, gail jones. (fourth row) thomas walker, mary anne gaye, jane edmonds, lois boston, fanny wiley, johnny waters. (fifth row) jackie mc neil, jackie walton, curtis patton, carol pindle, [illegible], milton reynolds. (sixth row) edward lord, richard thornell, leonard davis, richard ralston, marie jones. (seventh row) marvin tarpley, clarence tyler, jane anne johnson, grace brooks, joyce shakes, maris houston.

Fisk University Choir; Stagecrafters.

Dunn House Girls: Eva, Helen, Donnette, Barbara, Gloria (Niara), Jeanne, Jane, Ellena

Hildred, conductor; Front Line, Donna 2nd from L; Jane, 5th, Ellena, 7th, Barbara, 9th;
Second Line, Jacquie, 2nd from L, Maryann, 4th from R

AKA

Printed in the USA
CPSIA information can be obtained
at www.ICGtesting.com
LVHW010349211123
764492LV00001B/72